WOMEN
WARRIORS
Who Make it *Rock*

An anthology featuring transformational stories of

LOVE POWER & RESPECT

Compiled by Bestselling Author

NICHOLE PETERS

Women Warriors

Who Make It Rock

An Anthology

Compiled by Nichole Peters

Believe In Your Dreams Publishing

Women Warriors Who Make It Rock - compiled by Nichole Peters
© 2016 by Believe In Your Dreams Publishing.

These works are based on actual events. In certain cases, incidents, characters, and timelines have been changed for dramatic purposes in order to protect their privacy.

Acknowledgments

This book was created to primarily honor a guardian angel who is smiling down on me from heaven: my grandmother, "Essie" Peters. Thank you for always believing this day would come. I would also like to dedicate this book to "Maw Maw" - Mary Lena Thomas - please know Nijah and I will never forget you; we miss you so much.

I would like to recognize Broderick Curney, a real man who has shown me that, even though I have experienced so much pain in my past, I am a woman of worth. Your existence proves there are good men that desire love, companionship, marriage, and are willing to support their queen... You ROCK as a soulmate. To all my children whom I love with every drop of oxygen in me, Thank You, Thank you... Just know I am fighting hard to make sure you all have the best in life and are blessed. My position requires I take a lot of time away from family and I just want to say I love you all and appreciate the patience each of you have shown to me. I owe you all greatly and I plan on making it ROCK for us!

To Ma' Dear, the amazing Effie Peters, I love you so much, Mother. You have always told me to never settle and you had faith that I was capable of moving mountains. I thank God for blessing me with such a strong role model. To all my brothers and sisters, I hope you know that this baby girl is making history for us. Our family was once in bondage, but I am sure we will break every chain that's trying to hold us back. Ruby Lee, get well soon, baby, Sis misses you and needs you!

To my spiritual mother, Dr. Pamela Robinson, you are one rocking Woman of God! Thanks for always understanding life when I didn't.

To my godmothers, Hazel Harrington and Pastor Michelle Harris, God knows you two ROCK! Thanks for never giving up on me and keeping me full of the Lord's word. Regina Payne, you thought I was going to leave you out, huh? I love you too!

To my amazing forewords - Pasty, Rebecca, Rita - who are actually paying it forward in order to see others live with an abundance of Love, Power, and Respect, thank you so very much for your hard work and all that you do to see the next woman smile with a clear vision on LIFE!

A heartfelt thanks to the awesome co-authors in this anthology. Ladies, I'd like to express my deepest gratitude for your hard work, your patience, and your words. This is what makes America great... Unity, Love, Peace, Empathy, and Compassion. We are showing the world that when we use our POWER of LOVE, there is no force that can stop us.

I am also thankful to the professionals who assisted me in this project including my all cover artists team Maurice and Mario and especially, my two editors, Claudia and Jill. You two ROCK! Thanks for six long years of working together. I love you ladies.

To "The Motivational Lounge," let's get ready to rumble and make this book a bestseller. Thank you so much, team!

To Rebecca Hall Gruyter and Empowered Connections Network, thank you so much for giving me this amazing opportunity to have two TV shows on your own channel powered by VoiceAmerica. I appreciate you so much for noticing and seeing my vision!

To all of Father God's children across the world who have given me a chance or played a role in my life or success, thank you so much for your help. To every bookstore, book club, or reader, thanks for letting me share my story with you and also for adding me to yours.

Last, but not least, all the glory and honor goes to The Great I Am. Thank you, Father God, for blessing my family and my journey. Without you, nothing in this world would be possible. Me and mine will always serve the Lord. Amen!

*~ **Nichole Peters***

Table of Contents

The Breakthrough Warrior

Defining True Women of Love, Power, and Respect
Dr. Pamela O'Guinn Robinson

In 2012 Nichole Peters, one of my beautiful and extremely talented spiritual daughters, wrote her first novel, *A Woman of Love, Power and Respect – The Darkness Rises, Book 1*, in which she skillfully relates her story of the trauma and turmoil she experienced growing up in Louisiana's projects, Redmond Heights.

In the opening of the novel, she stated, "I want nothing more than for every young girl to grow to become A Woman of Love, Power and Respect." It is such a simple, yet profound statement, one that leads to this question: with all the ugliness and immorality of our world, how do we foster an environment for young girls that will promote and develop future women who represent love, power and respect? One thing is certain: Before we can pass on or even began to develop these attributes in ourselves or others, we must first have a clear definition and understanding of Love, Power and Respect.

In today's society, where tolerance for the once-intolerable is at an all-time high and everything that is wrong has somehow become the new right, how do we as a people truly define or even recognize a woman of love, power and respect? What are the true attributes of such a woman? Together, let's explore this topic in an effort to not only provide answers to the questions, but empower our communities with the wisdom and knowledge necessary to bring about a new generation of beautiful, intelligent women of Love, Power and Respect!

Love is often defined in many scholastic dictionaries as an intense feeling of deep emotion, or a romantic or sexual attachment to someone. Love has many variations depending on the object of the affection. The love one has for his/her mother is most certainly a different variety than that the individual feels for a romantic or sexual partner. Simply put, the world says love is about how someone makes them feel or how they feel about someone else. This is closely similar to these same dictionaries definitions of respect, which is described as a deep admiration for someone or something elicited by their abilities, qualities, or achievements, and it also means esteem, reverence, or to hold in high regard and to honor.

Yet God defines true love as being more about how you behave and treat others. It's not based on romantic or sexual feelings, but is a true reverence, care, and concern for others. It is a moral characteristic that encompasses much more than romantic fantasy could compare. Surprisingly, the worldly definitions of respect and the Biblical ones both refer to honor.

Now with this being said, let's look at how power relates to this and the importance it holds for us as women and, more importantly, as a people. Power is the ability or capacity to do something or directly influence the behavior of others or a course of events. So it's clear that these three characteristics are focused on and define how we relate to each other and the influence or effects of our interactions.

A woman plays a vital role not only in her family, but in society. It was a woman that God chose to carry life within her and to bring that life forth into this world. If she isn't a woman of good moral fiber and virtue, if she lacks in love and operates with no respect for others, she is a detriment to all those to which she is connected. Women are by nature powerful creatures and all relationships are infused by power. It is the passport to true intimacy, but only when it is partnered with love and respect, and once equally-shared and balanced, it creates happy individuals, strong relationships, satisfying marriages, and powerful communities.

There are many powerful women in the Bible from which we can learn, from Esther to Mary Magdalene and all those in between. What made these women different and stand out was the love they exhibited, the respect they showed to those around them, and the power by which they operated daily. These women, who all faced many adversities and challenges during their lives, understood who they were and whose they were, and refused to give up on themselves, their families, or their communities. Their commitments were unselfish and not based on romantic fantasies or misguided admiration or abuse of power. They gave love and respect freely and they understood the influence they had among people and behaved accordingly.

Being a female is based on our anatomy, and yet, I daresay that all females are not women and all women are not women of Love, Power and Respect. True love is not based on a feeling and respect is not to be taken for granted, just as power must be recognized and used wisely. Women have great influence in the lives of their husbands and children. Therefore, it is vital that they behave in a manner that produces and brings about positive attitudes, affects positive change, and nurtures the continuation of high moral standards and values.

In closing, I would like to believe that some valuable knowledge has been imparted to someone that was aware, that someone just made a decision to step up and become that walking definition of A Woman of Love, Power and Respect. If so, what is your definition of a Woman of Love, Power and Respect? More importantly, do you possess these qualities? Are you one that can join those of us striving to raise up a new generation of such women and leave the legacy for generations to come?

The

Purposeful

Warrior

Foreword
Rebecca Hall Gruyter

As a women's empowerment leader, I know a lot about being disempowered, but I also know how to overcome the lack of authority. I have learned how to gain power and step into the center stage of your life and SHINE - or as Nichole would say - step into your Warrior Woman and Rock!

I was so honored when Nichole Peters asked me to write the forward for *Women Warriors Who Make It Rock*, a book full of warrior women coming together to share their stories of overcoming hardships and stepping into their warrior power. In sharing their stories, these women will equip and empower you to tap into your truth and inner warrior. I believe this anthology is a living and interactive book that will speak wisdom, motivation, encouragement, and power into your life. Your heart will be touched and you will be motivated and inspired to take action to step forward powerfully in your life. I want to invite you to pause, take a deep breath, and be ready to receive these powerful stories and messages so they can ignite a fire that will give courage and purpose in your life to inspire you to take more action and SHINE!

The reason I'm so passionate about women stepping forward, sharing their wisdom, heart, lives, and stories is because I came from an extremely disempowered place. I experienced all types of abuse, from the tender ages of five until thirteen years old (my formative years), and I actually continued to visit that abusive environment until the age of eighteen. This environment of abuse taught me that "I am not okay"; that there is "something wrong with me"; that it must be "my fault"; and that it is "NOT safe to be seen or heard". When I was finally rescued by my birth father and placed in his home with my stepmother (who became the mother of my heart), I got to start my healing journey. On this journey, I discovered that these false beliefs I'd gained from before were actually lies. I discovered that I am beautifully and wonderfully made (just like you), on purpose and for a purpose; that I mattered and was needed just as I am; that it wasn't my fault; and ultimately, that it is safe to be seen and heard. So my mission, the calling of my heart, is to help others understand the truth: that we are all beautifully and wonderfully made and needed just as we are. When we step forward and share the gift of us, it makes a difference in our lives and in the lives of those around us.

I want to help equip and empower women to step into the center of their life - not just life as a supporting character or a role of some sort - but to really step forward fully in your life, to bring it all, to authentically and powerfully share your story, life, and heart with another. As Nichole would say, you will "Warrior Up" and step into your destiny. Some of the greatest gifts I have been given are by women who invested their life and heart in me. Pattie, the mom of my heart, used to let me follow her around everywhere and she invested her heart and life in me. We built beautiful memories and moments together because she leaned into me and opened her heart and life to me, showing me how a mother's heart can love and not hurt, but heal, hold, celebrate, and inspire.

I also have been blessed by my grandmothers (all four of them), who chose to invest their lives in me too. They shared their wisdom, love, life lessons, and beautiful traditions, leaving a legacy of strength, character, and loving messages that have healed, encouraged, and lifted up thousands of women throughout the years. They created the roots I now stand on, roots that go deep, weather storms, and which go deep enough and are strong enough to sustain the path I'm called to walk and not grow weary, to complete the race I'm called to run. I discovered life is not a solo journey. We need each other to encourage us, to speak wisdom and truth into us, to love us and cheer us on, and to help us stand up again when we fall. This book will walk beside you to help you run and not grow weary, to complete all that you are called to complete, and to SHINE (not just survive, but SHINE and ROCK it)!

Now it's your turn. Are you going to lean in and learn from the wisdom within this book? Will you let us walk beside you on your journey of life? We want to lift you up, support you, motivate, encourage, and empower you. But it is your choice. We want to help you grow deep roots that can weather the storms in life. You can choose to open the pages and let them pour into you, or you can put it on a shelf. My heart and prayer is that you will say yes to you and lean into the powerful messages and hope that are waiting to pour into you, your heart, and your life.

You all have unique gifts, talents, abilities, stories, journeys, and perspectives that you alone can bring forward. Those in your life need you, your message, your wisdom, your perspective, gifts, talents, and heart. You are a beautiful flower in the garden of life with your own fragrance, color, style, season, texture, and beauty that only you can bring forward. When we shrink back or hide, the garden becomes less vibrant and we all miss out. Be willing to share the gift of you with those around you and with the world!

You have already said yes to you (which I celebrate!) in purchasing this book. Now the next step is yours. Drink in the stories and messages that are within its pages to serve, support, and inspire you! Take the time to pause, read, and reflect. Listen to the powerful messages and hope that are waiting for you within its powerful pages. It's not an accident that you purchased this book and are opening it to read right now...today. I invite you to lean in and truly receive the messages and wisdom that will speak to your heart and soul that you will find in these Warrior Woman pages. Enjoy this rich collection of wisdom, love, and encouragement so that you can go forth in life, SHINE, and Rock!

Rebecca Hall Gruyter

Rebecca Hall Gruyter is the owner of *Your Purpose Driven Practice*, creator of the *Women's Empowerment Series* events/TV show, the *Speaker Talent Search™*, and *Rebecca's Money Summit*. Rebecca is the Network Director for VoiceAmerica's Women Channel in both radio and TV, is an in-demand speaker, an expert money coach, and a frequent guest expert on success panels, tele-summits, TV, and radio shows.

As the CEO of *RHG Media Productions™*, Rebecca launched the international TV channel called *Empowered ConnectionsTV™*, bringing transformational TV shows and programming to the world. She is a popular radio talk show host and #1 bestselling author (multiple times) who wants to help YOU impact the world.

http://yourpurposedrivenpractice.net/
www.facebook.com/rhallgruyter
www.facebook.com/pages/Rebecca-Hall-Gruyter/442052769207010
www.linkedin.com/pub/rebecca-hall-gruyter/9/266/280
www.twitter.com/Rebeccahgruyter
www.yourpurposedrivenpractice.net/speaker-talent/
www.EmpoweringWomenTransformingLives.com
www.EmpoweredConnectionsTV.com

A Warrior's Song and Purpose
Andrea Baham

Nichole asked me to write about how I became a Warrior. Hmm, where do I begin? Well, let me start with where I come from. I'm from the small town of Bogalusa, LA. I was raised by a single mom along with my five siblings. I don't have any personal memories of my dad other than stories that our family and his friends have told me. Growing up in a house with five sisters was a challenge, but we were taught one important thing, which is to always stick together. I learned how to be a Warrior from Mom. She was a single mother and had to battle other personal issues in her life, but she taught me to be strong, independent, and to never give up, no matter how hard the wind may blow. She also taught me that if I ever fall, I can always get back up and try again.

As I was growing as an individual, separate from my family, I learned quite a few things about myself. One of which was I was blessed with one of the most beautiful gifts God could give a person. I have the gift of song. Being able to sing astounding notes with my voice has been a comfort all my life. I can remember at eight years old, I'd be singing on the other side of the house. My mother would scream from down the hall, "Shut up all that noise, pea!" But I would keep right on singing. There was something inside me that made me happy and joyful when I sang. It was like something was moving on the inside and I didn't want it to stop. Not only did I fall deeply in love with singing, but I was in tune with all sorts of music. Isn't God good?

My mom would make me go to church every Sunday and I loved it because I was a part of the youth group and would sing in the choir. I can recall one Sunday when my grandmother was in the choir singing. I started singing along and everyone just started looking at me in astonishment. In that moment. I realized that what I possessed was special. After service, all the members surrounded me and told me what a beautiful voice I had. After that day, I told myself I wanted to be like Whitney Houston. I wanted to be the greatest singer ever. I was like a rocket that was shooting for the stars.

I've had many struggles in my life spiritually, mentally, financially, emotionally, and physically. It was around the age of twenty-five when I started to give up hope and face the reality that life hadn't gone the way I intended for it to go. I had been through a nasty divorce and I had to figure out how to take care of my three beautiful kids (Thomas, Trinity, and Isaiah), whom I love dearly. At the same time, I was struggling with trying to find who I was and my true place in society. I found myself in and out of clubs, I quit school, and at one point I felt like I had no one and nowhere to turn. I had given up completely.

I remember the day I was sitting in my truck with nowhere to go and I picked up the phone to I call my mother. When she answered, I began to cry and tell her how I felt and how lost I felt. She told me that I had to be strong and endure the storm no matter how bad the rain might seem to be falling down. In that moment, I vowed to myself and to God that I would be a better version of me and that I would always seek his face for guidance and strength.

I then turned back to my first true love: music! I began singing every Sunday in church and I started doing shows in local areas. I had been writing songs as long as I could remember and had a folder full of lyrics that I felt the world needed to hear. The lyrics have a story to tell and my music helps me express my feelings and tell my story of all the obstacles I've had to face and defeated.

Music gave me life and I have rekindled my relationship with singing. When I sing, I feel like there's nothing in this world that is greater and I see my dreams coming true. Music gives me a means of expression. It gives me a way to tell the world and people about my life struggles and the challenges I've faced over the years. It embraces and encourages me to set an example for other women who have been in my position. I look at music as my way out, a way to release some of the thoughts and worries I may be experiencing at times. Music is something I've been around my entire life and I think it's fascinating to see just how the words of a song can play a major role in the emotions people feel. I remember on many days my mom would sit on her porch and listen to blues or gospel, and I saw how it affected her emotionally, mentally, and spiritually. I realized I wanted to be able to have that kind of impact on others as well.

Even today I still go through many struggles, but I let my pen, paper and the words that come from my heart be my way to inner peace though release. God has given me a special gift and I intend to use it for the greater good of this world. My goal is to inspire others in a way they have never felt before, and I plan to do this through my music.

I take heed to my mother's words that I should get up, no matter how hard the wind may blow, and if I ever fall, I can always get back up and try again. I believe deeply within my heart that the best is yet to come, and God isn't through with me yet. For those of you who may be struggling in your lives, my advice is this: Never give up! Don't ever allow anyone or anything to stop you from trying. Don't let the weight of the world get on your shoulders or bring you down. You have to pray daily and seek God's counsel and be sure to keep Him first in all you do. Be sure to strive for greatness in all areas and aspects of your life. Regardless of how the situation may appear, ALL things are possible.

If you ever feel like you have hit a low point in your life, here are some ways in which I power myself up and lift myself up daily:

1.   Prayer and song. I love to sing and it can be a great way to feel uplifted and positive.

2.   Meditation. Sit back and meditate on all the things that are going well and working in your favor, and focus on your inner, individual peace.

3.   If you have children, use them to lift yourself up. Even when you don't feel like getting out of bed, they can give you the inner strength and motivation you need to get through your day.

I challenge the women who are reading this book to start touching more lives in a positive way. This world is so chaotic right now and we need more women who are willing to take a stand and truly start impacting some of the lost lives, because at the end of the day, *all* lives matter!

Andrea Baham

Andrea is a musical prodigy who sings, writes lyrics, and expresses herself through song to feel close to God and to help others. She sings at different churches and conferences. She is the mother of three children and believes that family is everything. She works in customer service, has a giving and kindred spirit. She has a crazy-fun personality and loves people. She plans on dedicating her life to music full-time soon and will build her career in 2017.

Remembering Nicole
Christine Hotchkiss

Each day is a new beginning, the start of another day, a new goal, a new attitude, and another opportunity to make a difference in my life and the lives of others. Each day I start with gratitude and continue throughout the day with compassion – not just compassion for the people who surround me, but compassion for life each day I am given.

I am a passionate woman who loves deeply and values life. I am also the reigning 2015 Ms. Triumph over Tragedy Queen. I am one of the strongest-willed people I know without having had support, guidance, or counseling to get through an emotional and life-changing event. I lead and live each day with a positive attitude and a compassionate heart by expressing unconditional love, happiness, and determination, not only remembering and honoring my late daughter Nicole's life, but keeping in mind the true meaning to what living life is all about. We all have a story to our lives and my story does not end because I am a loss parent. Rather, it is a new beginning to the life I choose to live and how I can help others appreciate life and live life after tragedy.

Tragedy

On New Year's Day 2007, my family and I were involved in a tragic off-road rollover accident at the Imperial Sand Dunes on the state lines of Arizona and California. Nicole was ejected from our vehicle and later passed away at St. Joseph's Hospital in Phoenix, Arizona. Amazingly enough, there were no exterior signs of trauma; however, her organs did not do well with the tossing of her body from our vehicle.

Nicole Marie Brown, my seventeen-year-old daughter - also known as "Coley"- was a blessing in my life. From the moment she was born, she was always smiling, giggling, and keeping everyone entertained with her ability to light up a room. There wasn't anything she wasn't willing to try or someone she wasn't willing to help. As a mother, my bond with Nicole and my son Austin are unbreakable and so are the memories I have. Nicole loved being a kid, and in a way, I lived my life through hers. She loved riding quads with her brother, skiing, driving go-carts, twirling a baton, playing the trumpet, and performing on the color guard team all four years she attended Centennial High School. She always volunteered "us" to go to the surrounding schools to recruit the new incoming freshmen to join the color guard. She had a passion to help children and decided she wanted to become a pediatric anesthesiologist. She and I volunteered at the Phoenix Children's Hospital, where she could get an insight on her true heart's desire. She excelled in her schooling from the day she began and it always amazed me how she would power study for exams the night before. I can't forget the big projects she would ask me to help her with that would be due the next day, even though she'd had weeks to complete it.

As parents, we are shut out of our children's lives because the mindset is "parents aren't cool". Not my Nicole! She and I shared many things, especially the girlie things. In 2005-2006 we competed in the Mrs., Ms. & Miss Teen Arizona United States pageant together, making it a memorable one for anyone who knew us. We didn't compete to win. We took it as an opportunity for personal growth, experience, and an awareness to our platforms. Little did I know that in my future, in 2015, I would compete and win at the age of forty-six for a title where my daughter was my platform. Nicole's platform was aiding the children at Phoenix Children's Hospital and I now had created a title all of its own being: living life after loss. Winning this title was an emotional journey, but my passion and determination to help others see life is still beautiful.

Triumph

You can triumph over any tragedy, especially after loss. The craziest, most unexpected twist on this competition was that two weeks prior, my thirty-six-year-old younger sister Lisa passed away in her sleep. I felt weak and strong all at the same time. My platform now had two angels near to my heart and God knew how much I wanted to continue my platform off stage as I had on stage. From this win, I have been able to open doors and have opportunities to aid and support people who are going through loss. You could say I have an angel on each side of me, guiding me, supporting me, and putting me in the lives of those who need my courage, strength, and compassion for life.

Anyone who has lost a loved one knows it is the heart that feels the forever void and the mind is always aware of a missing love and absence. Birthdays, holidays, and the day our loved ones passed have a different feeling and meaning. Over the past nine-and-a-half years, I have met some amazing people, listening to their life stories and how they either have found a way to celebrate life or assist others in celebrating life.

In the past nine years, I have found a more-meaningful way to express what celebrating life should be and is to me. The celebration of life is not the day we pass or the day we are born, but truly every day we are alive. The celebration of life is an understanding that there are so many things for which to be grateful.

Memories

Just as a birthday is remembered with a special moment in time, so is the day a loved one has passed, also known as an "Angel Day". Nicole's "Angel Day" is New Year's Day, also acknowledged for most as the first day and the new beginning of a year to come. But for me and my family, it is a day where we remember a tragedy that changed our lives for the rest of our lives, and the people who our lives touched theirs. For the past nine years, I have held a balloon release not only on social media but locally, where people come and share the memory of their loved ones. This is not just any gathering, but a Celebration of Life and to remember loved ones who have passed. Many people have come and participated in filling balloons, writing loved ones' names on each balloon, and releasing them at 11:11 to the song "My Wish" by Rascal Flats playing. That was not only my daughter's favorite song, but the words say it all. Not only do strangers, family, and friends come to remember their loved ones and establish new relationships, but I have each of them participate in writing a wish of their own on their balloon(s). I decided on this idea because with the tradition of us making promises or resolutions to ourselves, they can be quickly broken, whereas we never break a wish and we are always dreaming of more for our lives.

Along with my annual balloon release, five years ago, I, along with a good friend of mine who also lost her son, created a "non-holiday potluck" in the middle of December. Holidays can be the most difficult for anyone having a hardship or loss, and at that time of the year, we want to celebrate the meaning of Christmas and the beginning of a new year with hopes and dreams. But it is easy to get stuck in a state of sadness, depending on individual circumstance and state of mind. With loss, it holds a heavy weight on any heart. This is where my friend and I wanted to relieve the burden and allow other loss parents to come together to share stories and photos, and fellowship with others on the same journey. It has created some amazing support and new friendships, which is helpful to parents who feel they are alone. Truly, no one is alone!

The years have passed by quickly and not for a moment can I believe it will be ten years Nicole has been my angel, and not one day passes where I am not finding a way to share the true value of life, creating memories, taking photos, and having opportunities to help others in a time of loss. In the days ahead, I not only am working on establishing a day of recognition for all, also known as Celebration of Life Day, but I am working on a foundation that provides scholarships, aiding people financially to pay for a Celebration of Life event and an honoring burial for their loved ones.

Love Never Dies

All too often I hear the statement "I can't imagine" when anyone learns of my losses. At first, this was a statement I strongly disliked hearing because it makes for an uncomfortable conversation. But with that statement, I learned to "imagine" as others can't to teach people and make them see how amazing life is and how time is important. I don't have the magic words or specific steps in accepting the loss of a loved one, whether it be a friend or family member. What I do have to offer is this: Always look at what you have been given, not just the miracle of life, but the memories, pictures, and time you had with those you cared for. Every day is a gift, and in every day, there is a miracle happening. Life is precious and whether we live to be in our 80's or for only a few days, every moment is captured in time and should be valued. Everything is a choice. The choice to remember a loved one by honoring their memory with celebrations or with a cause is worth everything. I choose to keep the memory and legacies of my daughter Nicole and sister Lisa alive by being happy, being appreciative to what I had versus what I lost, and sharing who they were with others as I have done here with you.

My faith is what keeps me moving one foot in front of the other. Meeting other individuals who walk their own journey allows me the continued strength and courage to achieve my dream and goals of publicly speaking to others about loss and being a person who makes a difference - one person, one day at a time.

Don't let the things that happen to you keep you from being who you were born to be. If you are feeling low, you can power yourself up daily in these simple ways:

1.   Read and believe in positive affirmations

2.   Look in the mirror and say, "I am..."

3.   Create a morning meditation in which you say, "I am worthy of more than limitations."

"May you always have a smile on your face when your loved ones come to mind and a heart filled with love in the memories they leave you with."

Christine Hotchkiss

Christine Hotchkiss is not only a mother, but a caring and passionate woman who loves with all her heart and lives life to the fullest. She loves capturing memories through photos and sending encouraging and positive messages via social media and to every person she meets. She gives her time to people who need her strength, courage, guidance, and support. Christine dedicates her time by volunteering in her community, such as at St. Vincent de Paul's feeding the homeless. She supports many causes as well as participates in walks for cures for everything from breast cancer to the American Heart Association.

Her most-recent cause and passion is her determination in creating a Celebration of Life Day and creating a scholarship program to provide financial assistance for the cost of burial services. She believes you may not get a second chance to do everything you think will be there tomorrow. Her motto is this: Make a difference each day, one person, and one day at a time.

For more information, contact:

hotchkiss.christine17@gmail.com
http://www.facebook.com/azhugsnkisses.com

Love, Power, & Respect: Embrace with Grace
U. Lisa Williams

As we explore the concepts of Love, Power, and Respect, I ask that you think about how you may feel when there is a lack of healthy communication between you and others. I believe it is reasonable to say, we all want to be loved and respected, but there are times we have problems loving or respecting ourselves and other people. We abuse our power, so please remember to respond to everyone with love, power, and respect. Acting positively, whether it's toward yourself or others, reaps rewards that are loving, peaceful, and healthy benefits.

My Challenges

Over the years, I have survived some unspeakable challenges in my life that created a lot of pain, hurt, anger, and detachment issues. My mother was murdered at the age of thirty-one, when I was six years old and living with my guardian mother. The deplorable news shattered the lives of my sisters and me. This was only the beginning.

Throughout my childhood and early adulthood years, I had so much hidden anger inside, but there was no one I trusted to share what I was experiencing. My older sister didn't live with us, so I had to ensure my baby sister was not harmed by others. I also had to fight off people from inappropriately violating my body as well as fight bullies at school. I had to deal with the broken relationship with my uncle. These were just a few of the social issues I had to constantly deal with. In spite of the love and care they tried to give us, there were times when life seemed to be crashing down around us, and there were things my sister and I struggled with within the home, in our hearts, and outside the home.

Finally, high school graduation came, I stayed around for about another year then decided it was time to move on. I left the small town and headed for the big city, where I met my son's dad. Later I was abandoned by the father of my child and I felt horrible. Throughout the years, I experienced more challenging trials that would stretch my faith... at work, while raising my son, at church, and in the community. All of these negative situations can become overwhelming and can cause anyone to spiral into depression, but because of my foundation in God, this made life much more enjoyable and gave me the strength to move forward.

Loving and respecting ourselves and others can be difficult at times, because horrible things happen and we want to lash out. Many of life's circumstances we face, including the criticisms and stereotypes of society, block us from seeing how "fearfully and wonderful" made by God we truly are inside. I learned over the years, listening to others share their "why" to explain their misuse of power in which they do not love and respect others, that ninety-plus percent of the time, our reasons are similar: We have lost loved ones, we fear change, and we are angry or frustrated. Behind those reasons is suppressed pain and fear that shows "why" we do not love and respect ourselves and others.

I admit, these challenges ripped at my heart and sometimes my coping mechanisms were not wise: drinking, unhealthy relationships, overeating, and impulsive shopping. I was only harming myself. Hypertension, body aches, headaches, chest pains, insomnia, weight gain - the list goes on and on; girlfriend had to get it together. I had to change my eating and drinking habits, incorporate an exercise plan, stopped being so busy, and break away from some unhealthy relationships. Serving and seeking God saved me, even when I was slack applying His wisdom and backslid.

God's Word and Love Shaped Me

I changed from being a person who abused my power to a person who loved and respected myself and others because of two things. The first being my love for my son and the second being God's word. When I became pregnant, I realized my baby was a true gift from God. I remember saying to his dad when I discovered I was expecting, "It is no longer about us; it's about this baby. With or without you, he will be taken care of." I meant that with all of heart. My son means the world to me, and even though I raise him alone, God has always been there for us. Numerous times I felt broken, but love for my son and myself was always a motivator. Whenever the feelings of brokenness tried to weaken me,

I had to evaluate myself, regroup, and change my response to life's challenges. Giving up was not an option.

We all will be given tests at some point in our lives; however, the key to overcoming them is a combination of who we seek for assistance and how we respond to that help. Choosing ineffective solutions to our problems often determines the length and severity of the struggle. Many times I chose the wrong option to try to solve a problem, only to make matters worse, not just for myself, but for others, especially for my son.

I had to learn to call out to God and to read His word. I knew I was saved because God sacrificed His son Jesus. I am aware everyone has not accepted Jesus as their Lord and Savior and that's a personal, individual choice. I am also mindful that some who have accepted Christ still do not seek Him or God in their times of trial or struggle. This is a mistake. What I am clearly aware of and know is, if it was not for my relationship with the Father God and His Son Jesus, neither my son or I would not be here today.

Healthy Tips on Change

I learned that God loves us always, so see yourself as the Creator of all sees you! If you desire to get to the next level in every aspect of your life, I propose a few challenges for you.

1.   Self-Care - take some time to yourself! Set boundaries and leave time for yourself in your day, then follow-through. For example; if you decide nine o'clock is a dedicated time for talking on the phone, let no one alter that and learn to say no. Remember, it starts with you, and when you truly start loving you, you will see your future clearer, you will get the needed rest, take a long overdue vacation, and enjoy life "more abundantly".

2.   Find Peace - You need to be centered and have peace in your life in order to focus on your purpose. Living without true peace, means you are always scrambling around looking for relief from pain. I cannot imagine a life without God's peace, joy, protection, hope, and plans for my life.

3.   Love and Forgive - When we forgive and love ourselves and others in spite of failures, hang-ups, and set-backs, we are moving in the direction toward being victorious! Love and forgiveness plays an important factor in our lives when building relationships. Love frees you from anxiety and give you energy for helping others.

My wisdom does not come from the natural realm. I'm not saying I don't occasionally pick up a few nuggets from other people, but whenever I feel the need for more power, energy or strength to keep going, I constantly repeat one of my favorite Bible verses, "The joy of the Lord is my strength." God's Word is the only power source I can tap into that I know will help me power up and reaching out to God, my foundation; my spiritual wisdom keeps me going.

I never thought I could ever open up about my struggles; however, over time, I found myself encouraging others to press on with life, forgive themselves and others, and break away from some very serious situations. This is when my healing started. I realized that what I had endured did not hinder the discovery of my purpose in life. My testimony is powerful and has helped others going through similar situations. It was time to give voice to my untold pain, to reveal the unhealthy choices I made, and to share how I eventually soared over the trials and tribulations, so that others, specifically young women, may be encouraged if they have encountered similar challenges.

I hope something I share from my own life experiences, from situations I witnessed, and from the knowledge I gained from my spiritual foundation, will inspire and empower you to move forward in the divine predestined plans God has in store for you. I hope by sharing my story, this will empower, encourage, and lead others on the healing road to recovery so they can move beyond the pain, move forward, and triumph in their predestined purpose and plan for their lives.

I leave you with this: Believe in yourself! Life is precious. We must embrace every moment; resilience is vital. Remember, love is not abuse, lies, or selfishness. "You are loved, you are worthy, you are valuable, you are more than a conquer, and yes, you can do all things through Christ Jesus, Who strengthens you. You are victorious." No matter what you have heard or what challenges you have endured, know there is an unconditional, loving great plan and purpose for your life. Soar like an Eagle!

U. Lisa Williams

U. Lisa Williams is a compassionate, spirited, dedicated motivator, mentor, and community servant. She provides training for victims, veterans, and focuses on human rights, and effective communication. She served as a United States Army Veteran Sergeant and is the Founder/CEO of Tyler Williams3 (*Mediation, Notary, and Motivational Speaking),* Healthy Relationships Communication Services, LLC.

A native of Modeste, Donaldsonville, and New Orleans, Louisiana, she currently resides in Lawton, Oklahoma. U. Lisa is a nationally-certified Sexual Harassment and Assault Victim Advocate-Department of Defense, president of the first Lawton-Fort Sill Chapter of the Oklahoma Women Veterans Organization, and accepted into *"Women Veterans Igniting the Spirit of Entrepreneurship"* national program.

She holds a Bachelor's Degree in Criminal Justice and Organizational Leadership from Cameron University and is pursuing a Master of Arts in Human Services Counseling. She has received many exceptional awards from the DOD, United States Army, and community. U. Lisa credits her life, that of her son's Matt, and all her accomplishments, knowledge, skills, experiences, and abilities to God.

Webmail: twillinvest@gmail.com, womenvetslawtonftsill16@gmail.com
Website: http://heartofaneaglewarrior.com, http://predestinedtosoar.com, http://ulisawilliams.com
Social media links – FB: https://www.facebook.com/ulisa.williams
LI: https://www.linkedin.com/in/u-lisa-williams-51591834
TW: https://twitter.com/ULWms1/status/670018446315294720?s=17)

Self-Discovery: Love and Peace
Shawn Renee

Every day is a new day, and with each passing moment, I'm reminded of how blessed I am. To see the possibilities of overcoming adversity within this world has given me hope that all things are possible to those who believe. The beauty of wisdom has shown her face time and time again. What would we do without wisdom? That kind, old woman of wisdom has granted me solace while walking through life each passing day. She has held my hand and pointed me in the right direction. Thank you, beautiful wisdom, for you have never failed me, and in the depths of my heart, I know you never will.

There is a search that has taken over me without a fight. Truth awaits daily, drawing me closer and closer to death. When I die, it is my belief that it will be the moment in which I have truly discovered what really exists. Until then, I will continue on with each day that passes by to ponder what else is out there. Questions come to mind all the time. Who am I? Why am I here? Who should I help? What is my purpose? I have peace in the midst of these unknowns; they are what drive me to continue living. When I think about it, ignorance to a certain extent is a gift, for not knowing all has been the fuel of my resilience to live.

Up until the age of seven, most of my time spent living was without the company of other children. I learned to be content with just being. In other words, my existence in and of itself was what kept me occupied. The strong woman who had guardianship over me was my great-grandmother, and she was not one for words. Even so, I found nothing to complain about since a life of solitude was all I'd been accustomed to. I was blessed to feel my granny's love in many other ways besides conversation. I recall that each night she'd allow me to rest my head on her cushiony arm while sleeping. Her arm, a pillow that was the perfect temperature and the perfect size, in some way communicated to me that I was loved. I could sleep on it forever, but of course, eventually I'd have to wake up because my granny didn't tolerate sleeping all day. Granny looked upon staying in bed as being inappropriate, so each day I rose up to play alone.

On most occasions, I didn't play with toys because they were placed on a shelf out of my reach. To this day, I have no idea why she did that, but I can recall looking on the shelf at boxed dolls, wondering why I couldn't hold my lonely dolls. Didn't they belong to me, and didn't they need my love? Never did I speak of this longing to take my dolls down, since my granny was not the type of person to conflict with. I kept my mouth closed and learned to create my own world where I had the freedom to become whomever I wished to become. My inner world was indeed a special place for me then, and without a doubt, it is where I find comfort now. This inner comfort is what has helped me to cope with the many trials I've faced in life. It's what I call "peace".

Peace fills me up when darts are thrown my way. I continue smiling, basking in the fact that I'm blessed and highly favored. Peace is what is felt when no one seems to understand me but God in heaven. I feel peace when fear tries to grip me and all of a sudden I know that everything's going to be all right. There is absolutely nothing like the peace of God. No one can convince me otherwise. Great peace doesn't accumulate overnight, neither does it leave in that manner. It can take struggle, long suffering, hurt, and pain to learn to trust one's Maker enough to develop peace. When I learned to trust, I learned to love. Love is truly where it all begins. It is the key to insurmountable comfort and peace in life. There is much joy in knowing that because I have peace, my three children will inherit a measure of it as well. The understanding of that wonderful concept is indeed a priceless treasure.

Neither parents nor guardians can be effective in a positive light without sharing peace. Although my great-grandmother spoke few words, the one thing I felt from her was peace. While resting on her arm at night, I knew that everything would be just fine. I'm grateful that a measure of her peace was passed on to me. The powerful, positive energy of peace is strong enough to propel a child toward success even if very few words are spoken. On the other hand, if worry and doubt from a parent shows up in the place of peace, there will be no faith, and without faith, life is simply unpleasant and meaningless. Children are amazingly aware of things. They will sense a meaningless life, and furthermore, they will instinctively know whether or not they're in an environment lacking peace. The natural instinct of a child in that type of environment is to escape and it's highly likely they will eventually do so in some way or another. The question that hopefully comes to mind is, "Where does peace begin?" In order to impart peace into the lives of our children, it is necessary that we gain understanding as to how it's actually obtained. Peace has a codependency to love. It always begins with love. The more we love, the more peace we will accumulate. Love has its struggles, and through those struggles, peace is found. It is important to note that one must become proactive in protecting peace because it can and will at some point become susceptible to attacks. A small part of my own life provides an example of this.

The loss of my baby through miscarriage brought to my attention the unfairness of life. Negativity released into my positive world as a result of this. The only way I knew how to cope was to allow an exoskeleton to attach itself to my body. That exoskeleton was a protective mechanism to keep me from feeling or expressing love to a certain extent. I became cold. Strong love felt way too painful. At the time, little did I know that God had allowed me to experience such pain so I could grow in resilience and faith while ultimately leading to my complete trust in Him. Slowly, I felt my peace slipping away. Not realizing that my peace was under attack, I repeatedly kept asking myself, "What did I do to deserve losing my baby?" I thought I must've done something wrong, and there was no peace in feeling that kind of loss. Absolutely nothing calculated right. I found myself fighting love while replacing it with doubt, fear, and anger. Self-pity and depression began working their way in. My two children could sense their mother's lack of peace. It hurt me to think I was causing a disruption in the household. I knew I wasn't giving them what they needed. Their father would say, "Renee, you've got to get out of your head. Some things just happen."

I didn't believe him. Some things just happen? No, there had to be an explanation for everything. Nothing just happens. No one could understand or feel the pain I felt. No one could see me. I felt invisible. I didn't believe faith could move mountains anymore. My peace was suddenly dwindling away. I was under a spiritual attack. My peace was almost gone.

Never stop praying. Even when you feel peace leaving, don't stop praying. In the midst of the attack, I loved my family, and because of that, I never stopped praying. My prayers allowed me to feel love strongly again. With that love, I remembered that I had a purpose! I recalled knowing I was meant to do great and mighty things. My peace had been restored! The wonderful thing about peace is that it brings clarity of vision. I realized my purpose is to teach people about understanding who they are. With peace, everything became clearer to me. I'd survived the attack.

With having lived a life of loving, sharing, and caring for years, the experience of losing my baby showed me that though peace desires to stay, it's truly up to us to protect and keep it. Negative emotions will try to come - like fear, hurt, doubt, and shame, to name a few - and often the one that overshadows them all is anger. We have the power as to whether or not peace dwells in our hearts. The more we practice keeping it, the harder it will be to fade. From my own life experience, I would say the best way to do that is by giving love. Give love to your fellow man in the way God has blessed you to give. Some of the ways in which I give love is by being the best mate I can be to my mate, the best mother I can be to my children, the best daughter I can be to my parents, the best sister I can be to my sisters, the best teacher I can be to my students, the best friend I can be to my friends, and most importantly, the best worshipper I can be to God. Everyone has his or her own way of giving love, and giving love is our direct line to peace.

In my life, there have been many trials threatening my comfort, but with each attack, a discovery and broadening of the ability to love has taken place. I am stronger and more at peace because I made it through those attacks. Without them, I'd be caught up in the deception of feeling weak. I wouldn't know my own strength.

The ability to love without limitation is the most powerful weapon to use. Never allowing anyone or anything to restrict that love has been the ultimate gift to me throughout my very own significant existence. As I continue to love, my understanding is surpassed by the peace of God. Throughout life's journey, in peace I've discovered my calling. I shall continue to convey the heartfelt message of how special we as individuals truly are. The giving of that knowledge to others, in love, has brought about an incredible feeling of inner comfort. As life goes on, I will continue my endeavor in sharing God's love, and with that success insurmountable peace is inevitable.

Peace be unto you.

Shawn Thompson

Shawn Thompson is a certified schoolteacher, licensed hairstylist, certified Life Coach, Personality Hacker Profiler, and founder of SRT Education Personal and Corporate Development.

She is the mother of three children, and is blessed to have a beautiful co-parenting relationship with their father Tyson Thompson, a wonderful man of God. She resides in Tulsa, OK. Her belief is that we are all lifelong learners capable of personal growth, and her desire is to empower individuals with the knowledge of who they are, and most importantly, who they are capable of becoming.

"Education helps one cease being intimidated by strange situations."
~ Maya Angelou.

Love the Life You Live
Brandy Jones

As a single mother, I struggled with debt head-on, especially after my divorce. It was a challenge to manage my money and live within my means. My spending patterns were driven by bad habits like going shopping immediately after payday without taking into account that I needed to save. At the time, it didn't cross my mind to track my expenses and regular monthly payments. As a result, my daughter and I lived paycheck to paycheck. I was barely making ends meet and I was determined to keep her unaware of our precarious situation. My bottom line was always in the red and I never felt I ever had enough.

In those dark financial years, I believed that "money was the root of all evil". Yet, as I evolved in my relationship with money and gained abundance, I came to understand that this particular proverb existed to deter us from obsessive greed. I realized the knowledge of making money was more than gathering excessive material wealth; it was power, an energy that was meant to flow through us. Gaining this knowledge opened my mind, heart, and soul. I discovered a deeper truth: There is nothing wrong with waking up every morning **free** from worry about bills and basic needs. Money is but another tool to help us live well. Managing money consciously can assist in the attainment of goals, large and small, as well as help establish financial stability for generations to come, which, in turn, allows you to LOVE the life you live.

It is easier to say you love yourself and want to do right by your family when you take care of yourself and your finances. I became determined to prosper and not only make money, but to maintain and build wealth so I could be a better mother and a better me! It's important to understand that investing in financial stability is a testament of self-love. Responsibility doesn't necessarily mean you must sacrifice every pleasure. A person who loves themselves doesn't neglect themselves.

When you build upon financial wellness, you experience abundance. Budgeting means you've taken care of the business of living and are more available to create the life you want. Start by paying yourself upfront and putting a few dollars away with every paycheck. Then you can use that savings to pay for something unexpected that increases your joy and peace. Do something special for yourself, like spend a few hours at the day spa or check-off something from your wish list. There is no shame in treating yourself well when you manage the resources you have. Imagine enjoying a great vacation without worrying about funds, and coming home with money still in your pockets! Financial stability doesn't demand you to make six figures or more. It only requires smart choices. No matter where or when you are now...just start.

Embrace Empowerment

When we're having financial troubles, people tend to silently hide their feelings of insecurity, shame, guilt, and other negative emotions. We tend to think we are the only one making these mistakes and say, "I am the only one going through this." We judge ourselves as inadequate and feel disconnected, which is inherently not true. *No one is an island.* We all share common experiences, like being told success involves going to school for sixteen to twenty years. Most of us are told the only way to "be somebody" is to go into debt and have a traditional career. We all have times where we are worried about a lack of money and have expenses that drives us crazy, and that confusion only complicates our struggle. So, we need to accept a couple basic truths: 1) Life happens. 2) Money comes and money goes. With those truths, we need to consider that *how much money we actually have* is something not many people actually keep track of. Most of us blindly spend until there is nothing left.

Money education is not taught in our public schools, even though the school system is our common environment for learning. Why is that? Having an opportunity to learn at an early age about finances, credit, and how to avoid debt would be amazing. Knowing how to budget finances, manage money, and build wealth is an immensely-powerful lesson to learn in our society, but people from certain social-economic backgrounds lack these lessons that would positively affect our entire lives. People say learning another language is harder as an adult than it is for a child. As we age, people struggle to pick up new information and change bad habits that have become ingrained over time. I say to you, *it is never too late* to learn the language of financial fluency.

It took me years to admit I needed help in my relationship with money, which reflected how often I deceived myself. I hid from my financial truth, and not taking action for positive change became an emotional burden. I did not want to continue to pass that burden on, as we do without thinking, from one generation to the next. I wanted to stop the struggle and no longer hide from family and friends. I was teaching my daughter by example to struggle in silence. I now had another option: to be honest and open, and face problems directly.

In an effort to resolve my issues and to find a better way to manage my finances, I decided I needed to know more. I researched and acquired information on how to budget and save money. I created a strategy for addressing my creditors head-on. I sought out information and support from people who knew more than I did about fiscal health. Much like physical health, I started with one step. I found a steno pad in my apartment, took hold of a pencil and developed a willingness to write things down, honestly recording my earnings and what I was spending. I wrote down every detail of my income and my expenses: rent, utilities, groceries, clothing and school supplies for my daughter. After that, I began to partner with bill collectors I had previously seen as my enemies. I developed a simple plan to negotiate payments I could commit to. I designed a roadmap toward abundance. When I had money left over, I realized I had a choice to save it or spend it. I chose both. Two hundred and fifty dollars was deposited over the year into my Christmas Club Fund, a regulated place to keep savings separate, whether it was for Christmas or not. Being honest and taking action were the practices I implemented to gain stability.

Once I overcame my financial struggle, and wasn't constantly worried about a lack of money, I became more comfortable and opened up to those around me. Financially-stable people tend to be empowered people, and empowered people generally have more emotional security and confidence. For me, gaining financial stability allowed me to free myself of the burden of self-doubt. With this new sense of freedom, I became determined to share the blessing of confidence with others, by spreading the wealth of knowledge I had learned. When we put ourselves in a position to educate others, we increase the power of the collective. Philanthropy does not only apply to those with excessive disposable incomes. Giving back is a scalable practice that encourages empowerment. For example: If you save a hundred dollars each month with your system of clipping coupons, share that knowledge and empower others. Offer to get together with people to show them the best way to use coupons and save money too. With extra money freed up each month, individuals and families can reinvest in their lives.

Surrender the Struggle

Consider this simple fact: Taking care of your personal business, your family, and those who rely on you is not only a demonstration of power, it is also a demonstration of self-worth and respect. If you don't believe you can be successful, you avoid seeking advice on how to budget, save, invest, or manage money in a beneficial manner. If you tell yourself, "I am not smart enough," or "I don't deserve better," you won't be particularly motivated to effect change. How we feel about ourselves and how much we contribute to others are intangible goods worthy of investment. People who feel good about their lives, most of the time, have a high self-worth, while people who feel bad about themselves tend to have low self-worth and very little respect for themselves. Changing for the better and getting rid of bad habits is hard, but the feeling of confidence when you succeed in the goal to gain financial stability, is transformational.

When I was struggling to care for my daughter, my self-worth and self-respect suffered. I couldn't always get her what she wanted, but I tried. I remember, one of her favorite treats was going to McDonald's. On one particular day, she ordered the Big Mac, large fries, and a large soda. I had $5 and the bill was $4.95. I couldn't afford to get myself anything to eat after getting her what she wanted, so I lied and told her I wasn't hungry. However, rising to the challenge of providing a better future for my daughter proved to be the beginning of a lifelong strategy to raise my financial worth and respect.

One afternoon, years later, I was going through my wallet and saw several $5 bills that triggered the memory of treating my daughter to McDonald's with only $5 to spend. From that very moment, I began putting away every $5 bill that came my way. Now, whenever I get a $5 bill as change, I celebrate, and then tuck it away. This particular bill has become a symbol of strength and a reminder that I will always have an abundance and self-worth. I know I'm not broken, and I'll never be broken again.

Possessing a $5 bill is relatively rare thing because they don't come around that often. Most of the cash we carry are crisp $20 bills right out of the ATM, a handful of $1 bills or some change. So when you get a $5 bill, treat it like a jewel and a symbol for your financial and personal freedom. My $5 bills have, over the years, financed my Bucket Wish List. I have bought things like a beautiful double-strand of pearls and a hot-air balloon ride. My next goal is to take a trip to Australia and go on a walk-about. Those $5 bills have also bought things that have benefited me in ways people may not have noticed. I've been on spiritual retreats, attended personal development workshops, and read books that changed the fiber of my very being. All that and more, purchased with reproductions of Abe Lincoln's unsmiling face, adds to the tapestry of who I am. Woven in with the green-and-white threads of U.S. currency are new feelings of love for self, empowerment of self, and a healthy self-respect.

If you are currently in debt, know you will eventually get out of it. You have enough, right now, so start saving your $5 bills and help yourself accumulate enough money to knock something major off your wish list that won't take away from providing for your basic needs.

My business, End the Red, was born out of a need I saw of people who struggled with financial stability. I get excited working hands-on with clients because I can see the big picture, help them avoid pitfalls, and push them toward their financial success story. While they may feel stuck in the muck of life, pretty soon they start treading water, and eventually swimming across the lake of life. It's a slow process but I'm there to support them. In this partnership, they realize they are not alone. I'm there with them. I lift them up and tell them, "It's going to be OK."

Brandy Jones

Brandy Jones has always been an entrepreneur and educator. At the age of seven, she started her first business, which planted the seeds of her first savings account and thus began a legacy of financial empowerment. Growing up in a military family, she relocated often and became adept at building new relationships with ease. It is this instant rapport that her diverse clientele shares with her today.

Ms. Jones accepts where her clients are without judgment. Having faced her own struggles with debt head-on, Ms. Jones learned to negotiate with creditors, manage a budget, and rebuild her savings. She has walked in the shoes of being heavily in debt, and for her, filing bankruptcy was not an option. She wanted more than a quick fix.

Brandy Jones, CEO of End the Red, has a mission to empower others to live a financially-sound life, and her vision is to educate the youth of today to be fiscally-strong adults of tomorrow. Ms. Jones will assist those who are having difficulty with their credit and give them new choices through training and education. She has a unique way to get people to talk about finances, how they feel, and look at the big picture, and from there she can help them make sound decisions.

End the Red is a business where the client will feel empowered to continue to handle their finances in a more-responsible matter. End the Red's purpose is to provide clients with a very personal and educational path on how to budget, how to maintain control with credit, and how to develop a savings plan.

endthered.brandy@gmail.com
www.EndtheRed.com
www.facebook.com/5DollarsBecauseUmatter

This is My Truth -"He Kept Me!"
Lisa Nobles

I truly don't remember what exactly happened to me with the man who was supposed to love me and the piece of me that does remember is holding on for dear life! She's mad, she's angry, she's hurt, so how do you expect for me to get it right when I am wrapped in loads of frightening and daunting dismay?

Realizing My Truth

For two years or so, I remained in a state of denial and dissatisfaction because I began to believe what he told me about myself. Go figure, right? I believed, to a certain degree, that maybe it was a part of my doing, and to a point it was. After all, I deserved to be torn down and ripped to emotional pieces based on my hidden lack of worth, right? My crown of queenship became the crown of shame and self-doubt, but I wore it well. I was not enough for a man who was empty himself, and sadly, I was not enough for self.

You see, I lied to myself and I saw how damaged my perception of myself became. Unrighteous and indigenous actions on behalf of him along with blindness of relational bliss allowed me to turn a blind eye day after day, hour after hour, minute after minute, time and time again. My spirit was striving to convince my soul that I was, in fact, worthless.

I resisted my appetite of desiring ambition. I knew in my heart that reconnecting to the greater side of me would lead to becoming a better Christian, person, friend, possible wife, and family member.

In my broken heart, I asked myself, "Is this the time to accept what currently is, or is this circumstance my newfound normality and I am fighting a lost battle of sanity?"

Accepting My Truth

At this point, I began transitioning into a dysfunctional, unconscious conformity. I had to save my dignity, I had to protect me, right? The love of my life left me in order to marry his side piece.

When we forget the good within ourselves, seemingly all sight of victory vanishes as quickly as the passing winds of hurricane Katrina. We must search and find an inkling of greatness that leads back to modeling self-love, respect, dignity, and worth in order to remember who we were destined to be. Who you are at this moment does not validate who God is and can be in the midst of any struggle or circumstances. When we trust God, we become who we were ultimately meant to be: a warrior having overcome adversity.

I was looking for me inside of you because I forgot about me! I lost myself striving to please you and you never, ever, loved me. As a matter of fact, at that time, I confess, I did not even love myself.

Slowly the pain and hurt generated a heightened amount of chaos. Ultimately my hope turned into pain, my faith turned into fear, as cancer began to eat away at my insides. The fight that I should have had to rescue my dreams became an unleashed massacre of hell toward myself!

This Is My Truth

Being stuck is a direct result of allowing complacency and comfortability to set in and control our direction and passions and destroy our well-being. We lose ourselves when we are not careful. Additionally, we begin to give everything to everyone else, to become the status quo of human acceptance. We can become lost within the process of transition. We become victimized by our pain, which strips us of the uniqueness of being or becoming an empowered and enthusiastic warrior toward the growth and development of our future best self.

A victim mentality can make you feel as though you are in a P.I.T. (Place of Intended Trials). There will always be P.I.T.'s in life that will make us believe we are by ourselves and potentially aid in creating a victim mentality. It is imperative that we not reside in the P.I.T.'s of life tribulations because they are only meant to shape and mold us into the discovery of our God given purposes.

However, in developing a victim mentality, a painful experience finds a traumatized individual who has lost all hope and has simply given up on life.

We must be determined to find our power in our imperfections and within those paralyzing moments of agony. Within those decisions, we begin to live again. We will no longer be challenged with our past mistakes, but instead be revitalized and on our way to the road of emotional recovery.

To change that belief, one must first realize that change indeed is needed. We must accept that our lives require modification. It is critical to determine which is greater: the temporary feeling of mental suffering, or the possibility of unlimited potential. Some people can become victimized through their environment, and that responsibility is the collective reconciliation of humanity entirely. Either way, it takes time to heal emotional and physically damaged wounds.

Daily, he kept two homes - literally. I allowed him to leave me feeling as if my very existence was a mistake.

*I was under the impression that our dreams of becoming husband and wife was our top priority. **The Assumed** became my first name, with a last name of **Irrelevant.** Not only that, my permanent address was located at 0000 **Heartbreak Hotel Avenue**. WHAT? Mrs. The Assumed Irrelevant, 0000 Heartbreak Avenue, HB, 12345? Who does that?*

You may be thinking, "There is no way this could have happened to me; oh no, I would not have put up with that!" Yes, I knew in my heart, but the burden of proof resided only in the form of physical evidence and I needed verbal confirmation. I loved him so much and he could do no wrong – or so I thought.

Sometimes we have to spiritually die in order to become physically or emotionally revitalized. Life will weigh you down like bricks tied to your leg. Our souls can begin to sink fearlessly to a bottomless emotional P.I.T. What are you going to do when you see no way out?

Living Next Level

Sometimes we must give up in order to gain a new perspective about the wonderfulness of living again. When we are in search to fill an empty space in our lives, there must exist a mindset which aggressively searches for hope, joy, happiness, and peace.

Sometimes when we strive to be our best, we get into areas of life that tell us we cannot go any further. You have to learn how to fight in spite of, not because of.

Have you ever felt that you have no choice but to subject yourself to the here and now of the opinions, beliefs, and attitudes of others in a sounding world? Unfortunately, some are not willing to see that healing is found in the process of recovery, and in that process, the strength of a warrior mentality rises. Soar, my friend. Your beauty is waiting.

Silent prayers are rewarded and manifested when we rely on our Creator and begin down the road to self-forgiveness and love. The confession focus is not about me nor who I am or was. It needs to be about moving out of our own way in order to be who we want and need to be.

There is no growth without resistance. Yes, I said it! There is no growth WITHOUT the use of resistance. Resistance can symbolize resisting the need to remain in unhealthy relationships or unproductive jobs or resisting the need to settle holistically.

Living Our Next Level™ is a concept that invites life back to our lives when we defy the odds of simply existing. It says that we are in the process of overcoming fear, worries, and doubts that could S.T.O.P. (**S**lowly **T**ap **O**ut on **P**urpose) us from being true warriors of triumph and determination. Those difficult times of life, once confronted, should shape us into pushing forward with goals of living our best life!

We need to force ourselves to G.E.T. U.P.™ (**G**od **E**levates **T**hose **U**nder **P**ressure™) and reclaim our thrones of purpose. This is what I have found out, which has led me to the concept of *Living Our Next Level* ™ in life. When I am down, I can *will* myself to G.E.T. U.P.™ by the constant renewal of my thinking and purposefully placing my mindset on the development and investments in my goals and dreams.

I live on purpose and through purpose. I learn to live by faith in knowing that I am worth being successful, monetary gain, having the family of my dreams, or whatever. We must begin to realize, most importantly, that <u>G</u>od <u>E</u>levates <u>T</u>hose <u>U</u>nder <u>P</u>ressure™, which means that my strength has to be drawn from a higher source of existence. Even though things look terrible right now, I can and will get through it. At this point, I become determined to search for hope, peace, and self-love.

Resistance can foster growth and development so we should become the instrument and constantly purge non-empowering acts that are not designed to build us up. Resist negative self-talk and old friends/ partnerships that do not support your dreams. We must even resist ourselves by denying old habits to return that potentially limit us. You are actively rediscovering the value of YOU! YOU are unbelievable and YOU better KNOW it!

Find the courage to G.E.T.-U.P.™ by *Living YOUR Next Level*™ and reconnecting to the reasons you begin to dream initially. G.E.T.-U.P. ™ not by overlooking failures, but by resting in God's arms and trusting the process of renewal. At the end of the day, we are learning the importance of being thankful and grateful for where we have come. Take the chance of not allowing your past to *define* you; however, allow your *potential* to *ENLIGHTEN* you.

Become a student of Living YOUR Next Level™ by beginning to research warrior qualities that are found in others who have made it, warrior qualities that will help you to stay in a state of success by making good and strong choices about your life. Remember, our past mistakes do not validate us. We are qualified because we were CHOSEN and we have a particular warrior quality!

When God created us, He broke the mold and your contribution to the world can be as powerful as you set your mind for it to be. Live boldly and never forget where you came from. Never allow it to imprison your ability to be all that you can be. We are warriors, #livingOURnextlevels™!

Lisa Nobles

Lisa L. Nobles is an author, C.E.O, motivational speaker, and founder of Empowered Women of Faith & Purpose, Inc. The processes of change led her to believe in the beauty of the community and its unlimited possibilities. Being determined, Lisa realized, at a very young age, that every facet of transition, leadership, and business was an advantageous love affair with passion, hunger, and desire. Currently grinding to complete her Bachelor of Arts in Applied Behavioral Science, Lisa continues to embrace an enthusiasm for stimulating and educating individuals on purpose, passion, and determination. Her intentions are to inspire the world - one person and one family at a time.

Lisa has held several former committee positions with a variety of non-profits. Based in Abilene, Texas, they include Meals on Wheels board and the executive board of directors, CPS, NAACP, and I-Can! D.A.R.E. (D*istinctive A*ttributes R*equire E*xcellence) 2 Dream, and D.A.R.E. 2 be Exceptional, which was designed to encourage and train others on ambition, passion, and purpose. Lisa's greatest hope abides in sharing life's discoveries of transformative processes during the journey to self-discovery.

Connect with Lisa at:

www.facebook.com/ewofp
www.twitter.com/ewofp
www.ewofp.org
www.linkedin.com/in/lisanobles
lisanobles@ewofp.org

A Young Warrior's Purpose and Destiny
Ravin Robinson

As a stylist in the black hair industry, I have seen that healthy hair is a definite struggle that many African American women face from childhood. With so many textures, lengths, qualities, and styles of hair, it is very important that we learn to consistently and properly manage and maintain healthy hair in order to establish a more manageable relationship with our hair. If you are like me, hair plays a major role in your level of confidence and gives you the ability to express yourself and your style. There are so many options out there that help to camouflage the real condition of our natural hair such as braid styles, chemical treatments, wigs, and extension services - just to name a few.

Hair extensions, especially, prevent women from fully focusing on the health and condition of their own hair when they are not done professionally. Healthy hair is important because there will always come a point where we have to look at our hair and face reality and truth. Those truths are, that although there are options out there that help mask unhealthy hair, we should take pride in our hair by embracing our culture and treating our hair with the care it deserves. It is okay to try things. I am always trying the latest styles on myself and my clients, but I do my best to ensure my hair and my clients' natural hair is properly treated, moisturized, trimmed, and that I use the least tension possible in order to help grow hair longer, healthier, and more manageable.

I chose the name Beautii-Fulfilled's for my business. The name derived from my desire to encourage women spiritually and assist them in feeling confidently beautiful from the inside out. I believe that as women, we sometimes focus so much on our outer appearance and looking good that we often fail to realize that real beauty lies within. We all have a story, and I believe that hair is my ministry because I am able to encourage others while being inspired myself. As women, we sometimes need an extra boost in confidence, whether it be spiritual or physical, and I feel that I am blessed with a gift to help women discover their boost.

Growing up, hair, fashion and beauty were my thing. I was born and raised in Bogalusa, Louisiana. I discovered a passion for hair at an early age while watching my mom work as a licensed stylist for over ten years. Whether I was switching my own styles, watching my mother style hair, or playing in my family members', friends', or dolls' hair, I was always fascinated with the latest styles. I began styling hair part time from my grandmother's living room shortly after high school. Doing hair has grown to be my passion because I witness so many transformations - not only physical ones. Most of the time there are transformations from the inside out. I truly enjoy seeing women feel confident and it inspires me to give my best, knowing how much pride we take in our hair as women.

While attending the University of Louisiana at Lafayette, a close friend taught me the sew-in weave technique. From there, I discovered my talent for installing and styling weaves. In the summer of 2010, while home for the summer, I received a visit from my paternal grandfather, who shared with me the devastating news that he was ill and dying from cancer. Seeing him in his predicament, I placed things on hold in Louisiana, followed my heart, and met him in NYC, where I helped care for him until his passing in September 2010.

Shortly after the passing of my grandfather, I moved back to Louisiana. I enrolled in a local community college, hoping to pick up where I had left off. I began working part time at a gas station while being enrolled in classes full time and doing hair on my off days. Discovering a deeper passion for hair, art, and fashion, I was blessed with the opportunity to move back to New York, where I began to chase my dreams of modeling and where I also attended the American Beauty School in Bronx, NY. While attending beauty school, I worked as a student stylist at Love's Beauty, where I was able to gain even more knowledge and experience. Unsafe living conditions forced me back to Louisiana and I knew that this was yet another test to build my endurance and trust in God. Although everything seemed to be falling into place while in New York, I knew that obedience was better than sacrifice. I had to live more, overcome more, experience more, grow more, seek to love myself more, and be obedient.

In January 2013, I began taking classes again at the local community college. Back at my grandparents' house, I began devoting most of my free time to making a living doing hair out of my grandparents' living room. I later invested my money into purchasing a portable building with a portable sink, styling chair, mirror, dryer, cabinets, and air conditioner constructed by my late grandfather. I created the name Beautii-Fulfilled and began doing hair full time, devoting all of my time and energy into building my brand. I began selling hair extensions and offering monthly specials and I operated my very small business right from my grandparents' backyard. The building was unique and allowed me to connect with many women in a very private setting. I usually serviced one client at a time and discovered a woman's need for privacy, especially when it concerned hair. Privacy opened the doorway to communication, which helped me connect with clients on a more personable level. This built a more trusting and lasting relationship, giving me the ability to minister and be ministered to, and helped me to better understand client needs on an individual basis.

After almost two years, I was blessed yet again with an open door opportunity to move to Houston, Texas. I remembered being fearful of moving because things were going well in Bogalusa businesswise and I felt that every time I took advantage of an opportunity outside of home, something always led me back home. For that reason, I constantly prayed and contemplated, prayed and contemplated. I was with my family in Rosharon, Texas, and we visited a church. My mom had been encouraging me to move to Houston. I would be closer to the family and I would be able to grow my business. The sermon was about stepping into the deep and it encouraged me to have faith and not fear the unknown. I had been told that in order to succeed, one must be willing to take chances.

Knowing that God had my best interests at heart, I took a leap of faith and moved to Houston. A friend connected me with an office job, which was the doorway to get me there because two weeks later, I was blessed with a full-time salon position. Although all of my clientele was in Louisiana, the owner of the salon was willing to allow me to travel home one weekend every month to service clients back home. This was a major blessing and gave me the opportunity to grow my clientele and further my knowledge of hair and business while managing to keep my old clients. For months, I consistently traveled back home once a month, but soon it became exhausting and I decided to sell the portable building and focus on building in Texas while visiting

Louisiana every few months. Once again, things began to look up and everything seemed to be falling right in place.

In May 2015, I received the heartbreaking news that my maternal grandfather - the man who had raised me - had also been diagnosed with cancer and I feared the worst while hoping for the best, since I had witnessed this before. I traveled home frequently from Houston because shortly after starting treatment, my grandfather's health took a sudden turn for the worse. It was a blow of unexpected news, yet I trusted God and knew that whatever the outcome, me and my family would overcome it with God's help.

On July 20, 2015, one day after my grandfather's 55th birthday, my grandfather was called home. This was a very difficult time for me and my family because he was such a major part of each of our lives. For months, I remained home in Louisiana with family, traveling back to Houston only occasionally. I needed to take time to cope and support my family during this tremendous loss and focus on self-love while seeking direction from God. I spent time praying, reading, studying the Bible, and getting to know myself. I began to discover peace and realized that this was yet another season of endurance and proving that my trust was in God, I would not become a victim of circumstance.

In October 2015, motivated, I returned to Houston and, realizing my clients' needs for convenience in the city, I started the Beautii-Fulfilled Mobile Experience to satisfy hair needs in the comfort of their homes and offices. Little did I know that this would become a unique idea that my clients would truly value and appreciate and a definite way to grow clientele in a thriving city. My clients are usually very busy professionals, stay-at-home moms, working mothers/wives, college students, traveling women, work-from-home women, and women who simply seek reliability and privacy at their convenience. Houston is a very large city and finding the time to balance between work/school, family life, and salon time can be a hassle. I moved to Houston with no clientele, but I am beyond grateful to see major progress despite constant detours. I know that everything that happened was meant for my good.

I became a warrior through encouragement and motivation from others, but most importantly through the revelation that God's grace is sufficient. When I realized that situations in life happen with and without my consent and are most times out of my control, I knew that what determined the outcome was my reaction in how I handled these things. The hardest, yet wisest, thing to do was to keep going. I could have taken the easy route and given up, but I chose to keep striving as I work to execute each of my goals one by one.

You can become a warrior too! My advice to you:

1.   Don't be ashamed of your journey and don't be afraid to tell your story.

2.   There is always room for improvement in our lives, so never feel as if you have it all together. Life is a constant process of growth.

3.   Keep God as your "bestie". He doesn't judge. He listens, He understands you, and He provides you with <u>TRUTH</u> you're seeking.

Love, Power, Respect

The power of respect begins with each of us individually. In order to respect the people around us, we must first respect ourselves. In order to respect ourselves, we must first love ourselves. Once we love ourselves and respect ourselves, it will become natural to love and respect others through the power of acceptance.

LOVE who you are whilst passionately exalting your gifts and talents and pouring into the lives of others. Have the POWER to overcome fear by walking in your purpose and diligently seeking God for direction. RESPECT the process and know that tests will come, but persistence determines the outcome. Be a woman of Love, Power and Respect.

I challenge each woman reading this book to learn to love yourself - not only physically-your body or what you possess. Dig deep within and love the woman who you truly are on the inside. Rid yourself of every negative thought, feeling, and emotion you may have about yourself. Acknowledge past hurts and regrets that you may be dealing with. Admit your faults, face your fears, challenge your ambition, and take time for yourself to show yourself some appreciation. Pray consistently. Forgive yourself and admit your past mistakes. Forgive those who hurt you. Know that you are WORTHY regardless of the cards life has dealt you. Take a leap of faith and chase a new goal or dream and know that the possibilities are unlimited. Express yourself through your gifts and talents. Be uniquely you!

Ravin Robinson

Ravin's wish is to touch as many lives as she possibly can. She realizes that life, in the flesh, is very short so anything that she can do to leave a positive legacy is what she strives to do. She wishes to spread love to as many people as she can while fulfilling the purpose and mission God has set out for her to fulfill. Whether through her current business or future businesses, she wishes to inspire, encourage, motivate, counsel, give and show compassion, and although she has many business goals and dreams that she wishes to pursue and fulfill, this is her main goal in life.

To learn more about Beautii-Fulfilled please visit:

www.beautiifulfilled.com
Email: beautiifulfilled@gmail.com
IG: @beautiifulfilled
Facebook: facebook.com/beautiifulfilled
Appointments/Booking: www.styleseat.com/ravinrobinson

Honor Thyself, With Love, Power, and Respect!
Delonda Parks-Burns

Honor Thyself, with Love!

LOVE, LO-VE, Love is so amazing and very important, especially when you are gracious enough to know that you must pour it all into thyself first. I'm sure you agree, right? Well, I didn't know that back then, but I damn sure know that now. You know, when you're so busy with everyday life, you honestly don't give yourself the time to even sit and think about the importance of self-love - or as I like to call it, self-care. You can be so consumed with taking care of others, showering them with so much attention and love, that you completely forget about loving on thyself. How disrespectful is that? How selfish is it for others not to think you need love and attention too? That means the ones you love are self-centered people who suck the life out of you, without a care in the world.

I made a firm decision to not push aside my feelings. It is very important that we honor ourselves with love. Giving myself just a little bit more of me than I have in the past came from a place of me being sick and tired of being sick and tired of my situation. Being and living in a place of unhappiness caused me to experience pain and discomfort in my body, which was the worst feeling for me. There were many nights of pain dealing with arthritis in my knees and being overweight, which somewhat related to my knee pain. Also, I had to deal with working at a job and not really living up to where I think I should've been, which is living my dreams of becoming a successful writer, a successful businesswoman, and so on and so forth. I knew that, if I wanted changes, I had to connect with God most importantly, I had to reevaluate my life, and I had to get it together and, of course, honor myself with lots of love.

Understanding and honoring thyself with Love is so rewarding, and let me add, one of the best feelings in the world. Why, you might ask? Because you are taking care of you, and when you take care of you or when you're honoring thyself, you are in a wonderful place. You're happy, and that makes everyone around you...HAPPY! I pamper my mind, my soul, my body, and my spirit. All of that has to align, it has to work together in order for you to be happy and be well. That's rich, for me, it really is. Meditate on it, give yourself permission to honor thyself, however you chose. Just do it!

I take the time to sit with God. Praying is powerful. I pamper myself with a nice pedicure every once in a while, and I created a bath ritual. I watch what I allow to be put in my mind and watch what I'm putting in my body. I added some fitness and I always take some me time. I was never taught that, and I'm sure many of you haven't been taught that either, but when I made that firm decision - which I hope you guys also do - my life began moving in the direction that I want, and I love it.

I'm not expecting a speedy process; this is a lifetime journey. Honoring thyself with love is not something that you stop doing when you think your life is where you want it. You have to make it a lifestyle. For me, it's healing. I'm healing my life, I'm loving myself, and it's not selfish. It means putting yourself first for once. That's so important, and I hope you decide to honor thyself with love, like I did. You owe it to yourself, so go, do, and be great!

Honor Thyself, with Love Tips:

1.   Schedule some time to do something you absolutely love doing. Don't talk yourself out of it, even if you have children. We as parents, especially the mothers, will feel so guilty about leaving our children for some "me time". It's okay to take away from our little ones. Know that you deserve it.

2.   Create a nightly or daily ritual that allows you to have some peace, to have a clear mind, and get better connected with God. It could be taking a bath with candles and using your favorite Bath & Body products, soaking without distraction. Try to do it when the children are asleep if you have any children.

3.   Be careful of your words and be careful of your thoughts. Make sure you're feeding your mind with positive thoughts and speak life into your situations. Affirmation is amazing. Find some great affirmation and use them. They work!

4.   Be yourself, have your own mind, do what you feel is right. Stick with what you feel is right.

5.   Love on yourself daily. You owe it to yourself. Do you, feel good about yourself, and know that is a journey, so don't rush anything. God has you!

Honor Thyself, with Power!

Growing up as a little girl, I remember my godfather talking to me about how beautiful I was and how I was going to be a star. His words were always so inspiring and kind. My godparents had no problem having me at their home, especially when my mom wanted to go out or had to go to work. My godparents owned a farm, and I used to go pick peas with my grandmother and my auntie Dot. I will never forget it. Those times were the best time in my life as a little girl. My godfather was the male figure and role model in my life, and I loved him and my godmother dearly. I loved how much love they showed me. It was truly a blessing. My godfather's words gave me confidence, which to me is POWER! With that power, I feel like I can do anything I put my mind to. My godfather's words are planted inside of me, so when I feel like I can't accomplish anything and I just want to give up, I go within and remember that I'm a star and I have the power to accomplish anything I put my mind and heart into.

I've joined a business, which is going very slow for me right now. I quit before, but I had to remember what my mission was and that a quitter is not planted inside me, because I am a warrior - warriors never quit - and most importantly, I'm a star. My mission is to have 100 women in my Chicago community join me on a journey to live a happy, healthy, and fit life. I know some of you might be saying, "Girl, that's a lot of women." It is, but I have the power and the confidence to make it happen. Is it going to happen overnight? No, and I know it's going to be challenging, but I can handle it. I honor the power within.

Honor Thyself, With Power Tips:

1.   Daily affirmations will help. Speaking positive words into your life will help you build your confidence up, which will make you feel powerful. Get

some sticky notes, find some amazing affirmations, and place them all around your house. Who cares who sees them? Stay inspired. It really helps!

2.   Go to the library or your local bookstore and find books on empowerment or some motivational or self-help books. Reading helps me all the time and I hope it helps you as well. Try going to seminars and/or church. Being or getting connected to someone you look up to or can make a mentor can help as well!

3.   Sometimes you have to go within. Spend some time alone and have a powerful and meaningful conversation with God. He always has the answer. Do it daily!

Honor Thyself, With Respect!

When it comes to respect, it's absolutely important how you treat yourself. Disrespect yourself, and then guess what? You just opened the doors for others to do the same. I'm speaking from experience here. I'm speaking from being in disrespectful relationships with men in my past - all because I wanted to be loved by them and because I thought they loved me and were worthy of my love. I was unconsciously disrespecting myself, not knowing my own worth, and totally forgetting that I had the POWER! It took me so long, after millions of lies and consistently being cheated on over and over again. I'm sure I'm not the only kindhearted person who has forgiven someone who cheated on them.

One day I just decided that enough was enough after reading a book called *Mean Time* by Iyanla Vanzant. That book changed my life. It taught me how to focus on me and get connected to Spirit. After reading it, I told myself that everything I was going through was my fault and it was up to me to stop it.

And I did. I had to look deep within and become clear on what I wanted in life and for myself. I put my focus back on God because we always leave Him; He never leaves us. He comforted me through the process of healing. Once you learn how to honor thyself with respect, that's what's going to show up, which signals to people that you can't be disrespected. Be good to yourself.

Honor Thyself, with Respect Tips:

1.   It's so important to know who you are. Know your worth. You are worth so much more! You are a child of God. Get centered and get connected to God. He's the source to EVERYTHING! He makes everything amazing, if we only let Him...so let Him.

2.   Stop and pay attention to your life. If you are in a hurtful relationship, don't tolerate it. You don't have to. You are in control of how people treat you. Speak up for yourself and don't feel bad about doing it or else you're going to get pushed around.

3.   Make sure you value yourself. If it's something you know and believe in, stand by it and don't allow anyone to tell you how and what you should be feeling.

4.   Always work on becoming a better person. Work on personal development. Always be the best you can be. There is always room for improvement. Put 100% effort into what you do and watch how people respect you. Be the best you can be in any situation.

5.   Giving respect is so important as well. If you want respect, you have to give it as well. It's a give and take relationship. Take it seriously!

Delonda Parks-Burns

Delonda Parks-Burns lives and works in Chicago, Illinois, as a supervisor in the food service industry. She also joined Total Life Changes in May of 2015 as an Independent Wellness Consultant, where she sells an array of products to support healthy living, nutrition, and natural ways to relieve stress and maintain life balance.

Delonda's passion for health and wellness came from her own personal struggle with weight loss. She became tired of being overweight and dealing with all the aches and pain she experienced in her body on a day-to-day basis while also living with one kidney. When the aches and pains became so unbearable she couldn't get out of bed to go to work, that was the day she decided to take control of her life! So through her journey of self-education and finding natural remedies to assist with changing her lifestyle, she garnered an abundance of knowledge and decided to share her knowledge with friends and family.

Delonda is described as outgoing, loving, humorous, intelligent, aggressive, helpful, and caring. She believes that LIFE is beautiful and you should cherish every moment of it. Delonda is an avid reader who enjoys writing, going to the movies, dancing, shopping, traveling, and hanging out with my family and friends. She hopes to one day write her own bestseller. In her spare time, she also enjoys spending time with her husband and three sons.

Contact Delonda at: www.facebook.com/delondab

Become Your Warrior: Fight and Believe In Your Dreams
Nichole Peters

"The Lord will fight for you. All you need to do is stand still."

~ Exodus 14:14

My Ma'Dear always told me I was strong and courageous, a natural born fighter with a young heart. My older siblings assured me I was something different. They'd never seen a more determined personality. My grandma would smile at me with pride and say I would never settle. So I have always known I was destined for greatness. I was a super-heroine and a Warrior, capable of knocking down every obstacle, even though growing up I was an unlikely candidate for success.

History

I was raised in the projects of Bogalusa, Louisiana, a small town north of New Orleans. As a child, I was haunted by demonic nightmares that almost drove me to suicide. I experienced violence, mistreatment, and degradation from many people who were supposed to love, teach, and protect me. As a young child I would never forget the words of my grade school reading comprehension teacher when she told me my dream of being a successful author was doo*med.*

"Nichole, there's no way you can become a good writer. Why don't you consider a career that doesn't require any writing skills, because this is clearly one of your weakest areas."

She informed me of my supposed inadequacies with a smile on her face, as if she was helping me, but clearly she didn't believe in me. For seven more long months (it felt like years), I had to walk into her class. I hated it and her with every fiber of my being. Meanwhile, inside me grew a beast, a chaotic ball of self-doubt, anger, hate, and fear.

I discovered the demon that whispered, "Life is not worth living" in the dead of the night. As a teenager, I became more aware of my dysfunctional upbringing on my paternal side. For years I thought my hardworking Ma'Dear was my father's only queen. We had such a perfect family until it was shattered due to his unfaithfulness. I resented my father for years because of his double life. I refused to have a relationship with my father. The anger remained and the inner beast laughed and grew stronger.

In my community, some labeled me a "hot girl". A few elders would watch me outside with my radio, frown, and say, "She's always shaking her tail. She'll be pregnant before she graduates from high school, if she manages to graduate at all." All because I loved to dance my tail off. The evil voices mixed with those of the folks in my neighborhood, they whispered that I was worth nothing.

My grandma knew when I was feeling down. My Ma'Dear did too, but most days she was too busy working extra hours as a bartending supervisor, so there were times when it was just Granny. One day right after I'd started high school, we sat outside on the hot concrete porch and she tapped me on my shoulder. I was exhausted, just sick and tired, so when I turned around, I gave a fake smile. Granny grabbed my chin and pulled my face up.

She said, *"Nikki, look me in my eyes. So what, baby, if you are different than others? You are created from a different cloth, uniquely made the way you are for a reason. Accept the gifts Father God has given you. Others may have more book sense than you, but do they have common sense? Wisdom is the best gift ever. You don't even know how much wisdom you got at this young age. Until you know God's plan, start seeing the good in you instead of the weaknesses. I might not be here to witness all of your good days and works because I am getting older, but just know I will always be fighting for you, even in my angel wings. I will always be at your side. So promise me something, Nichole. Never let no human being belittle or tell you what you cannot do. You must fight hard in order to persevere. You will do it."*

At that very moment, I felt so alive. My will to survive was like iron shaping my spine. It was a hallelujah praise moment. My heart pumped hard and I shouted, "I can become a **WARRIOR**!" I started praying and that gave me hope.

God's voice was my confirmation that I would su

finished praying, I would hear the Almighty's voice t

message, my princess. Your purpose is straight ahea

prayers and my family's support, I managed to push

kept rising up against me and my destiny. I kept

graduated from Bogalusa High School on time without a ᵇᵃᵇ

college.

Despite clouds of total darkness, my struggles and my presumed promiscuity, I made it. That didn't mean I didn't falter. The inner beast wasn't conquered. I was so afraid to tell anyone about the horrific nightmares I faced for almost my whole life. After I prayed, the inner beast tore at my guts, made me curl up in despair. It would not let me give birth to the WARRIOR my Lord and family saw in me. It seemed the more I prayed, the more aggressive the attacks. So in a moment of weakness, I got tired of fighting, threw in the towel, and stopped praying to my highest power.

Big mistake! During the course of my life, I continued to experience more difficult challenges. I grew into a young adult who felt betrayed, powerless, and unloved. I had forgiven my father, and we were close again. He died when I was five months pregnant. I was only twenty years old, when any young lass would need their father's advice. My grandma, my HERO, was diagnosed with chronic heart failure soon after. She was constantly in and out of the ICU. Ten months later I lost her too. I was barely an adult and I couldn't think straight. I was drastically flunking almost every class in college, so I dropped out. I thought I had found the man of my dreams. Boy, was that a lie!

My biggest regret was I had fallen deeply in love with an undercover notorious drug dealer, subscribing to a life of dirty money, domestic violence, and sin. I ended up being abused and used. I became a single mother to disabled children. My children were born premature due to many factors, including chronic illness, stress, mental and physical abuse. By the time I was in my late twenties, I felt cold, destitute, and powerless. I'd made so many bad choices in my life by living in the fast lane. My health had even started to fail. But the darkness didn't win completely. I experienced so much joy along with pain. I never gave up hope.

...re my Nikki Woman Warrior tips for a successful, glorious life:

...iving into the beast as a young woman like to had destroyed my life instead
...leading to DISCOVERING MY LIFE'S PURPOSE. I'd stopped believing I
was a super-heroine and a Warrior. I was listening to all the negativity and
criticism from people who didn't care about me. Did I dare let the inner and
exterior critics who held the keys to my pain win? Never. My grandmother and
I never believed I would lose, so deep down inside I knew in order to grow I
would have to FIGHT! In order to fight off the demons completely and forever,
I needed to make major changes, but I didn't have the knowledge of how to
reinvent myself. I had to ask myself a question: how could I make a
transformational change? I asked God for guidance!

Spiritually Connected

In 2010 I became stronger than I ever could have imagined by realizing I
must listen to the right voices, not the inner demons. I had to focus on the
positive. I realized I was involved in serious spiritual warfare. I dropped down
to my knees and fell back in **LOVE** with my highest power, The LORD. When
you are totally connected to your Almighty source, your **POWER** from **The
Great I Am** becomes your greatest strength. I needed to stop running from His
message and make sure I delivered His message. Running away from speaking
life when you are chosen to help lead others will drain you, leaving you feeling
weary and in despair. Once I started speaking life to the masses, I felt good and
full of life.

You will be able to reinvent yourself by knowing the Power to heal you
requires a spiritual connection and love foundation. **RESPECT** it! Mentally
connected I started to ignore the negative thoughts and opinions that said I
could never become great as a writer, speaker, or A Woman of Essence. Once
I learned how to identify my biggest psychological challenges, I increased my
mental ability to become stronger. I was determined to stay mentally strong
despite gossip-mongers and haters. I learned the best way to "warrior up" and
fight mentally was to participate in positive support groups. Bible and Sunday
school, events, mixers, and spending social time with friends kept me sane. My
greatest accomplishment was when I became the Founder/CEO and a

bestselling author of A Woman of Love, Power, and Respect. I witnessed; I could tell my story and write about the struggle within. Your greatest battle is not only in your mind, but deep in your heart also!

Physically Connected

I grasped hold of myself spiritually and mentally, and all the dark clouds were finally clearing away to expose light. So after years of self-abuse, I was ready to get myself together physically. My passion was snatched from me for over two years because I was physically wounded. I couldn't help my children with their homework, write my books, or do any of my speaking events. I had been diagnosed with chronic diseases like hypertension and hyperlipidemia, the butt-kicking autoimmune diseases of rheumatoid arthritis, spondylosis, anxiety, neuropathy, and trust me, there were many more. I was in my late 30's taking over fourteen medications daily. I'd become a walking pharmaceutical zombie. I just couldn't stay focused. When your physical health is failing, you can become very ill and depressed. My income level dropped and I became dependent on public assistance again. You name it, I needed it. But not for long.

I've always wanted to live an independent life. I grew up all my life off the government. I lived in the housing projects for eighteen years. In order to feed my children, I had to depend on food stamps. I knew this generational darkness had to be broken. I wanted a better life for my children, so I put on my big girl panties and healed my body by holistic means such as deep meditation, becoming a top doTERRA Elite wellness advocate, hosting my own classes on essentials oils, and healthier lifestyle changes including yoga, eating organically, and taking plenty of natural herbal remedies. Now I am only taking sometimes four meds a day. Huge difference, right? Our health is one of our greatest successes we could ever achieve in a lifetime! FIGHT with everything in YOU!

Emotionally Connected

One may think being mentally connected is the same as being emotionally connected. But it is not! Emotions are chaotic and shouldn't be allowed to rule every action. How you handle yourself emotionally will definitely affect the mental, but understand emotions are fluid while your mental state should stay strong. I had a problem with allowing my emotional state to control me by focusing on my mistakes in the past. I had to battle my hurt, my anger, my frustration and fear. Staying focused on your past will keep you in a state of illusion emotionally. Start forgiving the younger you! Be not afraid. Do not fear what your critics, friends, co-workers, business partners and even some family members say. After all, no one can totally stop you from moving forward. When you own your emotions, they are in a good place. Watch the WARRIOR finally break through to position itself against the all naysayers.

Get Out of the Darkness

I mastered the art of containing the inner beast through so many trials and tribulations. There were horrible thoughts swirling in my head. The evil voices told me the Highest Power didn't love me. I would never be anything but a stupid, ugly, filthy rag.

Bullcrap! These negative thoughts had everything to do with me staying in darkness and refusing to forgive myself and others. The birth of the Warrior inside me reminded me of another voice. God's voice says to me: "I AM your Father. I AM WHO I AM. I will equip you in every way. Do not fear." I had to realize God chooses imperfect vessels to represent him. Even Moses dealt with inner demons and doubts. In Exodus 4:10 (NIV) - Moses said to the LORD, "Pardon your servant, Lord. I have never been eloquent, neither in the past nor since you have spoken to your servant. I am slow of speech and tongue." Moses listened to God's voice, not the darkness, and he accomplished miracles. My miracle? The great I AM said I would be an awesome speaker, and despite my disability, I have become a successful motivational speaker who communicates to the masses to women all over the globe.

Snatch Back Your Happiness

Joy is essential in your life. Let no one snatch your joy away. Do things that make you happy. My way of experiencing happiness is to let go and let God, even when a person does me wrong. When you don't forgive others, you open mental and emotional doors to bitterness and hate. Instead, focus on the positive. Keep your happiness alive by spending time with your loved ones, going out on family gatherings, going on dates, reading motivational books, writing, singing, dancing... I think you get the point. **Just Stay Joyous!** When you are happy, you feel and work better. Your passion comes completely alive. Be so happy it scares the hell out of you!

Believe in Your Dreams

Just know God wants you to be a glorious light. I am so thankful and grateful for my dreams coming true by sharing my work to the world. I witnessed people from all over the world telling me how my story has made a change in their lives. However, know that to fulfill dreams, you often have to sacrifice. You have to work hard and ignore those who hold you back. As I changed my old way of thinking and birthed my inner Warrior, I lost many people in my life. Boy, did it hurt!

It's hard to watch people turn against you because you're progressing. I promised myself and **GOD** I will never let anything get in my way on this earth ever again, and that means humans too! I realized I failed so many times because of negative energy. I refuse to take this into my 2016 journey and dreams. My passion won't let me. Once you set a goal and get a small taste of peace, positivity, passion, prayer, and prosperity, you will never go back to dwelling in misery with the demonic beasts within. I have witnessed the manifestation of my own dreams. Dreams that were realized when I was a small child have come into fruition. I am now in a place where I feel totally unstoppable and I am hungry to see others receive their blessing too.

Become your Warrior and fight hard through prayer, passion, and change so that you are a better person than you are today. Love yourself and believe in your dreams. There's nothing greater than LOVE! Make **LOVE** your greatest journey in helping others discover their passion!

Nichole Peters

Discover Your Life! Live Your Dreams! Love Your LIFE!

I am now the soulmate to an amazing man I love so dearly. He has shown me true love still exists. I am the mother of four beautiful, amazing children, and at forty-one years old, I am a Nana to one beautiful princess. I am a CEO and the Senior Executive of my blog talk radio show. I thank God for touching me with His amazing miracles to discover my life. I am living my dreams through His grace and mercy. If I can do it, you can do it. You must FIGHT! You are capable of any breakthrough. Let your warrior out to breathe so you can love your life. The **WARRIOR** in me battled back against every nightmare from my inner and exterior critics and has won! Nikki Woman was the black soul-sista version of Wonder Woman who wanted to save anyone who was going through distress and violence. The bracelet I wear every single day is truly my protection. It reads "GOD IS BIG ENOUGH."

WARRIOR UP!

The
Spiritual
Warrior

Foreword: Discovering the Warrior Within Winning Every War
Patsy Cole

Warriors are developed in war. I was born a warrior! I come from a family of warriors who know how to stand strong when the storms of life are raging. I often wondered why I experienced so many natural disasters once I embraced my role as a warrior. While on the battlefield I became afflicted and I kept silent. Some people unknowingly left me feeling like a "lone survivor", wearing the label "damaged goods". At times I felt as if I was detached from my very being - detached from everything that mattered to me. I labeled myself as the "forgotten warrior". The struggles, to a certain degree, almost ruined my life.

War Zone

"Faith, hope and love, But the greatest of these is love." The meaning of love is often misunderstood. Some define it as an expression, an action, or a language used to communicate feelings. Others have gone so far as to say that love is a temporary state of mind that slowly fades away.

At an early age I was taught by my parents that our Creator loves everyone. Long before I could utter the word "love", I experienced its benefits by being nurtured, clothed, sheltered, comforted, and protected. I'm so glad God revealed to me as a young girl that He is love and love never fails. I didn't realize it at the time, but that revelation is what would strengthen me while becoming the warrior I was born to be!

It was during my adolescent years that pain and sorrow taught me what "*love was not*". Prior to "Doomsday", my perception and understanding of love was that it was pure and innocent. But the detestable things performed on my virgin body left me thoroughly confused. Molestation wore a mask for two long years, impersonating as someone who cared about me. Although I was only 12, why didn't I recognize it wasn't love? It didn't feel like love, sound like love, nor did it resemble love. It was rooted in evil. I used to wonder why I allowed fear to silence me for thirty-six years until I understood that fear has paralyzing effects.

Boot Camp

I became a prime candidate for deception and my perception of love had become distorted. I was looking for love in all the wrong places: drugs, alcohol, disloyal friendships, and social environments. The few males I encountered *seemed* to be genuine and authentic. They even went as far as saying, "I love you." Sadly, every one of those relationships left my heart bruised and broken. Even counterfeit love has the ability to produce and that's exactly what it did...PRODUCE! I gave birth to my very first child during my senior year in college.

My status as an unwed mother was almost a stumbling block. Even my friends thought I would be the next college drop-out. There's no quitting flowing through the veins of a warrior. It's never an option! I had a legacy to leave in the hopes of impacting my family and the following generations. There was no time to retreat. So I put on my armor and decided to stay on the battlefield. Against all odds, I earned a Bachelor of Science degree. I'm a Warrior! Yes! I won that battle!

I knew if my search for love ended, my life would have little value. Surely there was a man on this planet capable of loving me like God loved me. Maybe he would find me. My past decisions did not reflect those of a royal position. Somewhere in the corridors of my mind I felt like molestation had murdered the princess inside of me. Nonetheless, I held on to the dream that Prince Charming was coming, riding in on a white horse to resurrect the princess with his love.

Shattered Love

The prince finally made his arrival. I regained consciousness and was able to breathe. Later, I stood at the altar saying those sacred words: "I do" and "Until death do us part." This relationship was eternal. All the other relationships failed because I wasn't in love; I was merely in lust. I gave birth to three additional children. There were good times and challenging times. The challenging times unfortunately outweighed the good. The ten-year marriage ended in what some would call a divorce. I call it "shattered love".

Love to the Rescue

As a warrior, I had suffered many difficulties: molestation, drugs, alcohol, single parenthood, and divorce. Although I survived, I was still a wounded warrior held captive by the pains of my past. I believed in a Superman. I truly thought he was coming to rescue me from the heartbreaks, guilt, and shame. I had deceived myself. There was no SuperMAN. He wasn't real. I didn't know a rescue mission was in operation and help was on the way.

Even the strong warriors become weak and have to leave the battlefield. The elements of surprise you encounter on the battlefield can drain the very life out of you. I needed to be rejuvenated, refreshed, and restored. Therefore, no matter what trials I faced, I never ceased going to my place of worship. I always gained strength from the sermons preached, songs of praise, and fellowship with other people of faith. I was then able to refuel and prepare for the next assignment.

Once again I stood at the altar. The last time I was there, I made a vow which I didn't keep. This time was different. I was DESPERATE! A warrior is loyal and honest. She embraces the quote, "To thine own self be true." I stood at the altar admitting to myself, confessing to God and others that I was in bondage. I was enslaved to unforgiveness! The person I needed to forgive was the one I stared at daily in the mirror: myself. Every warrior knows the power of a "war cry". The words that I shouted from the depths of my soul were these: "I want to be free!" It brought me victory. The true warrior in me was being unleashed.

Power Outage – One Warrior Down!

A warrior understands that fighting is inevitable. Sooner or later on this stage called life you will have to engage in combat. Therefore, it's necessary for the warrior to enlist in training. This provides skills needed to ensure a victory. It also prepares you for the various attacks and strategies of the opposing forces. The utilization of weapons depends upon the type of battles you encounter. However, in every case, there's a proper way to use a weapon. Improper usage could cause injury or possibly death.

I can recall going through an extensive reality-based training session. I was successfully working in corporate America, prospering in most areas of my life.

It had been a few years since my relationship with Prince Charming ended. I not only experienced the unleashing of the warrior, but my ability to dream had been restored. I was given another opportunity to share with someone my failures, my success, my love, and my life. This time he wasn't a prince, but he was crowned with all the qualities of a king. I wasn't seeking him out. He actually found me. I was in my warrior position, displaying good character in the midst of chaos. I never believed in love at first sight, but there was something about this man that attracted me to him like a magnet. I wanted so much to ignore his invitation for a relationship, but my warrior instincts wouldn't allow me to reject such an offer.

After spending only three months with who I believed would one day be my king, I experienced a surprise attack to my body. The doctor's report diagnosed me as having fibromyalgia, an incurable muscle disorder. Please allow me to say, it is the disease from hell! The news definitely caught me off guard. I had been hit with many blows but I always got back up. This one literally knocked me off my feet. As stated earlier, this was my reality-based training. The pain was real. The depression was real. The losses were real and the FEAR was real. Warriors are supposed to be courageous. It would be an insult for me to allow fear to paralyze me again. I was no longer bound. I had been set free!

Those two years were full of misery one could not imagine. Although I experienced the above-mentioned emotions, I was able to maintain my status as a warrior. I had the mindset of a warrior that victory would be mine. This time I wasn't alone. I had a man by my side who also possessed a warrior mentality. He knew I was a warrior and he utilized the weapons of patience and endurance to help me endure this battle. It was a struggle just to get out of bed each day. Some days my bed became the battlefield in which I had to fight against hopelessness, distress, and despair. I had to endure tormenting thoughts of suicide. It was at that moment that I declared, "This means war!" I reached into my arsenal and pulled out my most POWERFUL weapon.

War Room

I fully trusted in the power of prayer. After all, God's miraculous power was first seen in creation and it was by His power that the world came into being.

He gave men the power to achieve things they would not have been able to accomplish in their own strength. I was convinced that I, too, had been granted this same power, but God's supernatural power and wisdom was mandatory in order for my body to be healed. I had many enemies to contend with for my healing: doubt, fright, panic, dismay, and my greatest adversary, the devil. I was determined to be healed!

I was fighting to get my life back. I had lost my job, my car, my house, and temporarily lost my children. The warrior in me knew I could not lose my mind!

Mission Possible

I was on a mission! My bed became my war room. I prayed to God morning, noon and night - when I felt like it and even when I didn't. There was another war going on in my mind, telling me that I was losing, which ignited something in me to fight even harder. I was fighting the fight of faith and defeat was not going to be my demise. My Warrior King was still right by my side, believing in his Warrior Queen…believing in the power of prayer. I was inspired during prayer to change my diet, start an exercise regiment, and consume natural supplementation. I implemented each of these on a daily basis and two months later, I was pain-free… completely healed!

The wounds received during my mortal combat experience created in me a "warrior mentality". I concluded that warriors are designed to sustain injuries. I was hit many times by enemy fire, but with the help of God, I always found my way back to safe territory. The battle scars I wear today are a constant reminder to me that I've been hurt, but I'm healed. I'm being made whole.

Today I am an educator, a minister, a mentor, and a Certified Believe Therapist. I married my king and have served as his queen for eighteen years. My assignment is to recruit and train other women to become warriors - women who make it rock.

Respect

Self-respect and respect for others is a warrior's honor code. In addition, the warrior knows that when you stand confident in your own worth, respect will soon follow.

Warrior's Decree:

I am a warrior by divine design. Therefore, the weapons I possess are those of mass destruction and "No weapon formed against me will ever prosper." Every battle loss is preparing me to emerge as a victor. I am winning the war and taking no prisoners! I'm not Superwoman. She doesn't exist. I Am a Woman of Love, Power, and Respect.

Patsy Cole

Live...love...laugh is not just her motto. Patsy emulates this on a daily basis. She intentionally embraces each God-given day by expressing joy to all those she encounters. As an advocate for the disadvantaged, Patsy longs to see others transformed from feelings of inadequacy and insignificance to lives of confidence and influence.

She discovered the intentions of God for her life in 1998 and accepted the ministry call to "Do the work of an evangelist." Due to her traumatic past of childhood molestation, FEAR attempted to sabotage her destiny. However, in 2006, Patsy defeated the odds and became the founder of Be Made Whole Ministries, which focuses on holistic healing of the spirit, soul, and body. Its purpose is to empower, encourage, and equip others to move beyond their painful past and present challenges into a purpose-driven life.

Patsy holds a Bachelor of Science degree and is a member of Delta Sigma Theta Sorority. She retired from her position as a middle school Science/Bible instructor after eighteen years. As co-author of *Phenomenal, That's Me!*, *Still Standing, Positioned 2 Prosper: Eight Golden Nuggets to Ensure Your Prosperity*, and *Discovering Your Destiny, Loving Your Life and Living Your Dreams!,* Patsy's desire is to lead readers down a pathway to wholeness. As the co-host of *A Dose of Trinity* radio show, Patsy has also appeared as a guest on radio and television platforms. She has a published article in *Run On* magazine and is excited about the curriculum publication to be used during her *Free to Be Free* workshops, pre-launching 2016!

As a mentor, Patsy's compelling passion to empower women and to help hurting humanity is ever-increasing. A sought-after conference speaker and workshop facilitator, she takes the hope and healing message to religious and secular audiences. Her passionate delivery, sense of humor, and transparent heart captivates and delights people of all ages, genders, and backgrounds. Each message is rich with Scripture, real-life stories, candor, practical steps, and relevant analogies. Her presentations shine with clarity and engaging illustrations while stirring the hearts of those who seek emotional and spiritual freedom.

Patsy, a native of Mineral Wells, Texas, and mother of five, resides in Arlington, Texas, along with her loving and supportive husband of eighteen years.

"I've had many giants to contend with, however, God has not allowed me to be overthrown by any."

Contact info for speaking inquiries:

www.facebook.com/evangelist.cole
www.twitter.com/PcmCole
bmadewholecenter@yahoo.com
www.linkedin.com/in/patsycole
www.bmadewholeministries.org

Running your Race with Love, Power, and Respect
Melinda Walker

Women warriors, it's time to run a race towards glory. II Timothy 2:5 says, "If a man also strives for masteries, yet is he not crowned, except he strive lawfully." I Corinthians 9:25 says, "And every man (woman) that striveth for the mastery is temperate, (has self-control), in all things."

Love, power, and respect are three key components we all need to finish strong. Love is to have a strong liking for. We have to have a profound, tender, passionate affection for the race we are running. We have to take pleasure in every aspect of the race. Love suffers long, beareth all things, believeth all things, hopeth all things, and endureth all things. Love will give you that push to follow through until the end. Love will make you run in all types of weather. Love will give you strength when you are tired and want to give up. Love will make you strive lawfully (do right) when you are tempted to do wrong. Love is the glue that gives you the stick to it when you would fall into pieces. Love never fails.

The best love is the kind that awakens the soul and makes us reach for more, that plants a fire in our hearts and bring peace to our mind. Power is the stamina that will help us endure the long period of time it takes to run a race. When we have power, it constitutes us against all outside interference. Power is having the ability or the capability to accomplish something. Power releases confidence. When we are confident, we have full trust and belief in ourselves. We run in our lane and we run the race that is set before us. Power helps us to rock steady and keeps us focused on the prize.

I Corinthians 9:24 says, "Do you not know that those who run in the race all run, but only one receives the prize?" Run in a way that you demonstrate with high regards that you want to win. We have to demand respect. When we run in such a way that shows we want to win, respect is earned. Your opponent will know you are in it to win it and then you will earn their respect. Love gives us the passion to run. Power gives us full trust and belief in ourselves, and when we hold the position we are running in the race with high regards, we earn respect.

In a race, the runner comes dressed in light-weight clothing. It is hard to run efficiently when weighted down. Women warriors, anything that is in our lives that weighs us down and may hinder our race, we have to lay it aside. We cannot allow jealousy, unforgiveness, anger, envy, strife, or any other such thing to relinquish our love, power, or respect. As a runner, we have reached our starting point. The starter tells us to get on our mark. He is saying, "Place your feet on the place where you will start." Joshua 1:3 says, "I will give you every place where you set your foot." Women warriors, some of you are marking the beginning of a new start for you and God is ready to give you the territory that you mark. The starter says, "Get ready, get ready, and get ready!" It is time to take into account the last race you ran. It is time to capitalize on all your mistakes. It is time to count up the costs and consider all of the 'what if's' and realize there are ups and downs. You have to tell yourself, "I may stumble and fall, but I am getting up and getting back in the race. I will not give up and I will not grow weary. I will endure 'til the end."

The starter then says, "Get set." Our minds are made up. I am setting my face like a flint; I will not be moved. I will keep my eyes straight ahead. I will not look to my right or my left. I am focused on the finish line. I am positioning myself. It is so important for us to be at the right place at the right time, wearing confidence and demonstrating high regards for the game. Expressing a profound, tender, and passionate affection with fire in our hearts awakens the soul and makes us reach for more.

I am reminded of the story of the rabbit and the turtle. They were opponents in a race against one another. The rabbit was fast by nature and the turtle was slow by nature. The odds were against the turtle and he had slim to no chance of winning. The rabbit had everything ability-wise that was needed to win, but he lacked the character. He exhibited speed, but he was running all over the place. He didn't have discipline and he was out of control. He was confident he was going to win hands down. The rabbit had several opportunities to win, but he did not take the race seriously. He then became complacent and decided to take a nap while the turtle was slow, but sure. The turtle was focused and consistent. The turtle did not let time intimidate him. He did not allow the attempts of the rabbit to distract him. He kept moving. He made moves in silence. He never took his eyes off the prize. He moved in quiet confidence and he wore it well. The rabbit slept too long. When he woke up, the turtle was crossing the finish line. The rabbit took for granted the power of consistency. Steady won the race. Let us take note of the turtle. He was slow but sure. The rabbit was fast, but he did not last.

It is not ability alone that will allow us to finish strong. Our character will sustain us when our ability cannot. Our gifts, talents, and abilities will get us there, but our character will keep us there. We have to do the right thing because it is the right thing to do, even if no one is looking. We have to have those qualities like the turtle, interesting and unusual. Love, power, and respect are qualities that are interesting and unusual.

To be a good runner, you have to exhibit leadership qualities. You have to be willing to run the distance. You have to be physically fit and mentally tough. Long distance runners are rare because it will take stamina to endure long periods of being uncomfortable. You have to have fortitude and some stick to it. In order to run our race with love, power, and respect, we have to be able to perform at own best regardless of external conditions, distractions, or internal emotions. We have to know distractions are going to come from without and within, but we have to keep our eyes on the goal. Every good runner anticipates their opponents' next moves and takes advantage of any opportunity of weakness. The goal is to win, but also the goal is to run the race with love, power, and respect. If you want to be a good runner and succeed, you have to have resilience: the ability to bounce back from adversity, pain, or a disappointing performance. We have to stay focused from all distractions. We have to exhibit strength and have the ability to handle any unforeseen turn of events and remain calm. We have to have preparation and anticipate situations ahead of time. We have to have vision. We have to see ourselves at the finish line, even when we do not see the finish line. We have to be open to new possibilities and have to have that trust in our ability to hold up no matter what happens on the road we are traveling.

As a good runner, there are many qualities we must possess, but in this chapter, I will leave you with three main points. The race that I'm speaking of in this chapter is the one that centers on you fulfilling your God-given purpose. Life will throw us many stumbling blocks, but we have to know how to deal with every circumstance in life as a good runner. It is not about how fast we run or how far we run, but it is about finishing our race. We have to run in such a way that we win. Love, power, and respect are three key points that we should take note of.

Three points of love to take note of:

1. Love beareth all things.

2. Love believeth all things.

3. Love hopeth and endureth all things.

Three points of power to take note of:

1. Power gives us confidence - full trust and belief in oneself.

2. Steadiness and consistency is the fuel to our own power.

3. Power is the stamina that gives us the ability to accomplish our goals.

Three points of respect to take note of:

1. Hold the race with high regards. Respect our race.

2. Respect the lane we are given to run.

3. Run the race in such a way that will earn respect.

Melinda Walker

Melinda Walker was born and raised in Bogalusa, LA, the younger of two girls. She joined the outreach fellowship revival center in 1993 and has been serving there ever since.

She wears many hats. She is a mother who supports every aspect of her children's lives. She is a wife who helps and supports her husband in his business and in ministry. She is a servant in ministry who teaches a Sunday school class for the primary and secondary ages. She has been ordained as an evangelist and is the choir director who serves the community in many aspects.

Her ministry serves the people of Jefferson Davis County and surrounding counties. It serves and encourages at the senior assisted-living convalescent home. They air a radio broadcast on Sundays from 7:45 until 8:15, where she has been speaking for many years.

Her life is centered on serving others, whether it's helping others with their FAFSA or motivating them with her words. Her life goal is to have an experience with someone and enhance and make their life BETTER!

You can contact Melinda at:

www.twitter.com/melindawalker
melindawalker73@yahoo.com

Under Construction
Rita L. Taylor

When I was a teen, I would often feel not good enough or not pretty enough or light-skinned enough to fit in. In my private time, I would do things such as pretend to have long, flowing hair, imagining that I was from somewhere far away. I was like many teens of today, thinking that things like wearing designer clothes and wearing tight skirts would make me feel like I was a part of the in-crowd. My dad was a pastor, so it was very easy to smile on the outside, all the while feeling very empty on the inside. Being a part of the church, we had practiced appearing to have things all together. Something kept tugging at my spirit, forcing me to be true to who I really was. There were times when I took part in things that were not a part of my upbringing. It left me feeling guilty and ashamed. I could never really fit in, even when I tried my hardest.

It wasn't until I began to search the inner core of who I really was that change took place. I began, with time, to realize I had a desire to succeed. I began to strive to be all I could be, even with a failed marriage and the embarrassment that came along with it. I made a declaration that I would be who God had called me to be. With all of the negative in the world, you have to learn how to turn all negative energy into positive energy! One key thing for me was I had to accept where I was, embrace my flaws, and allow people to be people. We are all under construction; there is always room for improvement. I'm a firm believer that we as women need each other to survive. What we have been through should not stop us, but it should encourage us to bind together and be a testimony to any and all women who may be traveling our route. Everything I had experienced in life was not for me, but for the testimony to others. *I WAS CREATED FOR KINGDOM BUILDING.* That was liberating.

It is very important to bind together as women, showing love to one another. By doing this, we can build a nation. There's no room for separation. We have to make sure that we are constantly building one another up in love.

As a body of believers, we have to be ready to serve. We have to be different, set apart, unique. We have many different roles we play. Our purpose in the church is kingdom building. Our purpose in our homes is to be the best mothers and advisors we can be. Lastly, in business, we should operate with the utmost integrity.

I remember at times I was angry for no reason at all. I wore a smile on the outside, but emptiness and anger on the inside. I traveled at the time with an award-winning celebrity. Life appeared to be good. My mom and dad provided a loving and nurturing home. However, the material things did not change my stinking thinking. What some people didn't know was that I was a very unhappy individual. One thing that made me smile was my children. I lived for my kids. I attended all football games, cheer tryouts, choir concerts, and of course, basketball games. Taking part in my children's extracurricular events made me feel worthy. It provided me a place to belong. I was so secure in my suburban lifestyle that I felt nothing could penetrate the wall of security I had built for me and my children to abide in. My attitude was that I had it under control. It was my perfect world.

It wasn't until I got the dreadful call from my boss that all of that changed. We are very close friends and our boys were college roommates. At 2 a.m., any parent would shake with fear upon hearing the phone ring. I answered the phone with a shaky and trembling voice. In slow motion, I heard my boss' voice say, "Rita, Roy has been shot!" I remember not focusing on anything else he said. I believe he said, "It's not looking good"

I tossed the phone receiver to my husband. I began to walk the house shouting, "Jesus! Jesus!" In my mind, all I could think about was getting to my son. My mind was going faster than my steps. I thought, *Is he okay? Is he alone? How could this be happening to me? I sheltered them from all of this. How can I get to Tyler, Texas, from Mansfield, Texas, in five minutes? My son needs me.*

I called my sister Terri. She knew how to drive the highway carefully and hastily. Upon hearing the news, Terri was at my house in a flash. She got me to Tyler in record time. Terri turned an hour-and-forty-five-minute trip into forty-five minutes. I didn't know what to expect. My stomach was in a knot the entire trip.

When we arrived at the hospital, my son had just gotten out of surgery. The receptionist told me to have a seat and the doctor would be with me momentarily. It seemed as if I was waiting for months. When the doctor finally approached me, he seemed concerned. He grimly informed me that my son was in grave condition, that they'd almost lost him two times in surgery. He also informed me that Roy, my son, would probably never walk again because of a bullet lodged in his leg. The bullet had severed a major artery and the blood loss was tremendous.

As the doctor spoke, my knees got weak. I could no longer stand so I took a seat. I could not help wondering, why me? I didn't bother anyone, so why was this happening to me? As I walked into the ICU, a doctor met me at the door and told me Roy couldn't hear me. With every step I took towards the ICU, I began to grab hold to more faith and change how I would react to what I saw.

When I approached the bed, all I could see was tubes everywhere. I could hear the sound of the respirator taking every breath for my child. I experienced a "now faith" moment. I needed to see a move of God immediately. I whispered, "Roy, this is Mama. I'm here, son. If you can hear me, move your leg."

Just then the doctor interrupted and said, "Mom, he can't hear you." I repeated myself and said, "Roy, this is Mom, and if you can hear me, move your legs." Roy began to slightly move his legs. That was a sign to me from God that He still had the situation in His hands. I was overjoyed.

We stayed in Tyler for thirty days with my son. Every morning I would get up and pray to the Father. I had gotten away from prayer because, in my own way, my life was too busy with doing things for my children. I needed an attitude adjustment. I began to change my thought process as it relates to the truth and the facts. The fact was my son was in ICU from what could have been a fatal gunshot wound, but the truth is Jesus is a healer.

Roy is twenty-seven now and has minimal scars from that dreadful day. He has made a full recovery. My faith is strengthened because of it. I embrace the fact that my attitude is not always right. I also embrace the fact that I have to change the way I view things. I still had to go and see my son in a grim state, but after my personal prayer and praise and worship, I saw him healed, walking and recovered. Sometimes we get so overloaded with life that we shut the world off. We feel like we have control over our daily situation. Events will happen to shake us back in position and bring our Superwoman attitudes into perspective. We all need reminders from time to time. We need an attitude overhaul.

I found that removing myself from negative things and people helped me to have a better outlook on things. We all have bad days when things seem disorganized or disheveled. Try changing your thoughts. It will change your day. I have discovered that if we change how we view a situation, it will make a huge difference in the outcome. What we think about becomes who we are.

With all of the things I have been through, I know God was shaping me to be a minister, a publicist, and a personal assistant. Whatever your dreams are, don't let life's happenings detour you off of the Master's route. No matter what has taken place in your life, it was for a purpose, to build character in you for the journey. Don't abort the process.

Let God Chisel You

A chisel is a sharp tool with a sharp edge. It's used to carve into something solid, something stable and consistent. God will cut away all that is not ordained in your life. God is the potter and we are the clay. God will, through life's adventures, mold us and make us to be all we were designed to be. Chisel all negative things away for purpose. God knows the plans He has for us, that of good and not of evil, to bring us to a known end. We can't take shortcuts to reach our destinations. We have to follow the planned process.

Follow the navigation. God preset it. If you so happen to falter, God will be there to re-route you. When setting your navigation in your car, it sometimes takes you the long way, but it knows about traffic or danger ahead and recalculates the route for you. Allow God to navigate you to that beautiful place in Him.

We may not be where we want to be…but glory to God, we are not where we used to be!

God has made a lifetime investment in each of us. We live life with God's purpose in mind. We are not purposeless!

Kingdom construction means binding together to build God's kingdom. Our actions and words should always be to build up and encourage one another. Sometimes we need to reconstruct our attitudes and change how we think. God is always working on you! Let God do the necessary repairs, fix-ups, and reconstructing in your life.

Women, know that you are impeccable individuals. Every day that you live you are faced with unexpected adversities. I would like to impart into you a few "Ritaisms" that I have made a part of my soul. If followed and implemented, they will guide you to be the strong confident warrior God has intended you to be!

1.   Years ago I took a CPR class. One of the first things we were taught to do is to assess the situation, then react. This is the first "Ritaism". When faced with adversity, we must first and foremost assess the situation, then positively react. Sometimes it is hard not to immediately react when faced with adversity; however, I want to encourage you to always step back and assess where you are, assess what is going on, assess why something is occurring in your life at this time. Carefully think about your response, and then take positive action. Remain positive and begin to change your thought process concerning the negative events that enter your life. This mind God has so blessed us with is a powerful thing! If we think negative, we receive negative; however, if we impart positive thoughts in all circumstances, even though it may look dismal, the outcome creates an atmosphere of positivity. Warriors, remember, it is mind over matter.

2.   The second "Ritaism" is simple: Always put a plan in place and execute the plan! Most of the things in life we encounter are things we have heard of or dealt with from the past. By having this plan in place, it helps us to look forward and execute the plan. Warriors, having a plan is of no effect if it is not executed!

3.   Which leads us to the third "Ritaism": Surround yourself with positive people! We have enough empathizers and sympathizers on our side. We need people in our lives who believe in us and celebrate us. We must have people in

our lives who encourage us to keep moving and keep us accountable. My son plays basketball and one year he was on a team that it seemed could not win a game no matter what combination of players they used. A true fan never loses hope in cheering for the team they believe in. It was our responsibility to keep our team uplifted and remain positive in the midst of their losing. After a few more games, this positive atmosphere we created caused the team to begin winning game after game. They eventually won a tournament championship! Seek out people for your life who will cheer you on and encourage you while you are faced with adversity. This positivity will help you as you walk into the calling for your life!

Mrs. Rita L. Taylor

I'm a native of Fort Worth, Texas, and the second child of five born to Bishop Willis and Lady Rita Pace. I have been married to my husband Pastor Christopher F. Taylor for 25 years. I have six beautiful children: Christeyun, Roy, Ashleigh, Christopher, Matthew and Trystan. I have two grandchildren, Ryleigh and Jaxson. I gave my life to Christ at an early age and have been tirelessly working on the battlefield since that time. Besides wearing the hats of wife, mother and grandmother, I have been a key figure in the secular arena; such as operating the Princess Boutique Charm School, which mentored young ladies ages 13 and up, teaching etiquette, and sustaining and building healthy esteem and morals; co-founder along with my husband Christopher of the Agape Christian Learning Academy.

I hosted a radio talk show called "Inside the Heart with Lady T", which was an open forum discussing pertinent Christian issues. I have served as the personal assistant to David and Tamela Mann, also known as the Browns, where I handled their personal and entertainment business. I am, along with my husband, the co-founder of New Direction Ministries, which is a healing ministry which offers Christian servanthood training. I have served as a pastor, an armor bearer, a counselor, a publicist, a mentor, a spiritual advisor, a teacher, a true prophet, and a friend. My ministry serves as a conduit to heal hurting and weary women. God has blessed me to be an influential pillar and an anointed vessel and powerful preeminent voice in the kingdom.

I am a woman of profound intercession, coupled with a passion to heal hurting people. Do not be fooled by my quiet, calm demeanor for I am one of God's generals, yet, I prefer to operate in humility from the back! I am first and foremost a worshiper! I am therefore very confident of my calling and my assignment in this 21st century. I stay reminded of Jerimiah 29:11:

"For I know the plans I have for you, declares the Lord, plans to prosper you and not to harm you, plans to give you hope and a future."

Put On the Warriors' Execution Routinely
Dr. Lisa Baxter

I grew up in the beautiful city of Fort Lauderdale, Florida, among Caribbean parents and 10 siblings. My father was recruited from Jamaica to work in the cane fields of Belle Glade, Florida, whilst my mother, Bahamian decent, had aspirations of becoming a nurse. I was the baby at the time which launched my mother outside of the home into the workforce and my father to bear the responsibility of caring for me.

Through the night, as a baby, my father nursed my chronic earaches and restless sleep disorder. My sleep disorder was so acute that the doctors prescribed a drug to relieve the restlessness. During that time my father had no other choice but to take me to work with him. In the mornings he would visit our local community store and treat me to my favorite pecan swirls. However, this would shortly change when I fell from a ladder trying to accompany him on the roof. To his astonishment, I'd managed to reach the top stair, only to plummet several feet to the concrete. To add insult to injury, he'd hired a neighboring woman to nurse me, but rather than nursing me, she abducted me – which caused mayhem, and resulted in a community-wide alert.

By elementary school I'd acquired a speech impediment—triggering my normal speech to become a profuse stutter and mute in most classroom settings. Weekly, I was taken out of the classroom with a speech pathologist to develop my skills in communication. It is apparent that the prescription I was given as a child had major repercussions and would later haunt me for a period of my life.

Although we were advocates in the church and my father had built several in the community, by high school, my developmental growth was compromised and I'd acquired an addiction to barbiturate-type drugs. During this time, drugs had infiltrated our community and I was introduced to alcohol and marijuana/cocaine. Although I was functional and a recipient of various academic and athletic awards, as well as becoming the first Black homecoming queen at a predominately White school, my life took a spiral downward turn for the worst.

The 80's hit the scene and the Jamaican posse was in full force, taking control of our community and I was one of the targets. Drugs appeared fashionable; everyone seemed to have their hand in the cookie jar. One particular day, I'd seen this sporty-looking car, cruising down the street to drop someone off. There was a mysterious looking silhouette behind the dark tinted windows. Each time I'd see the car, the person inside would make a flirting gesture by driving the car towards me. I later found out it was my brother's ex-girlfriend Wanda's new boyfriend.

One morning, after a long night of binging with my girlfriends, Wanda's brother (Kenneth) asked for a ride. Initially, we didn't want to be bothered, but decided to give him a ride anyway. After a few moments, Kenneth came back to the car motioning us to come inside. Of course, we felt a sense of eeriness but decided to take him up on the invitation. Shortly afterwards, drugs and this mysterious person appeared simultaneously. Naively, I thought he liked one of my girlfriends, but once he'd left the room, they insisted he had his eyes on me. To my dismay, they were absolutely right. We soon found out the mysterious guy's name was Omar and he drove the mysterious car that had been flirting with me all that time. He made a deal with my friends and paid them to follow us as he made his move. That move would cost me more than I could bargain for.

Did I mentioned I was engaged? My finance Brandon, was stationed in Europe at the time and sent for me, provoking the short meet-and-greet to fizzle out rather quickly. However, inundated with Brandon's unfaithfulness and the physical altercation with his secret lover—at our place of residence—I returned to the States immediately and Brandon quickly followed suit. (Of course he caught these hands).

Once in the states, Brandon apologized and we began planning for our wedding. One day, sitting at our community park, Omar appeared. And although Brandon and I were planning our wedding, Omar swept me off my feet with drugs, lavish gifts, and sports cars. I was "hooked, lined, and sunk", battling with the decision to marry Brandon. The day before our wedding, I told him I couldn't do it. Of course, this didn't go over too well. He cried and whispered a few words I will never forget, "No one can love you like I love."

To this day, it's perhaps one decision that caused a rippling effect in my life for many years.

I decided to marry Brandon anyway, at our residence, while Omar surveyed our wedding from a distance. Conversely enough, it wouldn't be a week before the marriage was annulled and I was whisked away to Jamaica by Omar. He wined and dined me, took me to the most lavish hotels in the island, but it didn't come without a price. I was quickly thrown into a whirlwind of police corruptions, gun violence, betrayal, womanizing and much more.

Next, I was lured into altercations with his women, especially his baby's mother. She pulled a gun on me, punctured my tire, and became pregnant, which was the last straw for me. On the other hand, I retaliated by throwing a deadly missile in her car, nearly killing her and her infant child. I would admit I didn't know the child was in the car, but I was totally out of control and arrested shortly afterwards. Later on, I would miss my court date and served a warrant for my arrest. When I did arrive to court, I was shackled as a common criminal. It took the death of a friend being shot in the head at gunpoint and a prophetic dream to risk the chance of leaving Omar for good. I ended up with my parents in a rural place where it was peaceful and quiet. I received a call from a coach regarding a scholarship to South Carolina. It was an athletic scholarship in three areas, basketball, softball, and volleyball. Without question, I took the scholarship for all three and thought I'd escaped my dreadful past once and for all… until Omar found out where I was.

Omar removed me off campus involuntarily, uttering, "If I can't have you, no one else can." Of course, that boosted my ego; besides, why would he travel so far with his posse if he really didn't love me. That was the routine — fight then make up. Which is exactly what went down. A little drugs, money, and a promise of a Jaguar and new home did the trick for a struggling student in college.

Little did I know, the Federal Bureau of Investigation (FBI) was tracking his every move. This particular morning, I had an early class, but received a call that my sister was stranded in North Florida. Being the liberal sister that I am, I asked Omar if he would take me to give her a ride back to school. He agreed and we were off. However, before hitting the main highway, we stopped at a convenience store, and I stepped out of the car, leaving my purse behind. Put a pin right there.

What takes place next would tarnish my life forever. As we hit the highway, I fell asleep, but the acceleration of the car woke me suddenly. Swiftly approaching the Florida state line, Omar was in a high-speed chase with the police. All I could remember is the car accelerating to the point of vibration. Our lives were at stake! Omar sped around cars, off the road, into the median, and on the highway again. I pleaded for him to stop but to no avail. Within moments we were in a hot pursuit. Once Omar finally stopped, we were surrounded by police and heavy artillery. My hopes of graduating and playing sports on a collegiate level were shattered in a million pieces. To add insult to injury, Omar placed drugs in my possession. Remember, the purse I'd left behind? Well, that same guy who lavished me with elaborate gifts and dreams placed drugs in my purse!

Cocaine was placed in my possession, along with cash and a firearm in the glove compartment. I was arrested and faced life in prison, ultimately sabotaging my family's respect and honor. After a couple of weeks, my father found out I was jailed and immediately headed to the police station to bail me out. But… it wasn't that easy; they wanted me to turn State's evidence. In other words, they wanted me to testify against Omar.

Needless to say, I did not "turn State's evidence" and the bond was finally set. My father bailed us out but it wouldn't be hours before Omar masterminded a scheme to skip bond hearing. This meant my father would lose everything! Although he'd mentioned paying my father back, the damage was done and I didn't trust him at all. It took my FATHER to draw the line. Labeled as a fugitive too? That didn't quite go over so well in the family. I left Omar and shifted to North Florida.

"Whose report are you going to believe" bellowed from the pulpit of a renowned ministry while in church one Wednesday night. "You will not serve one day in prison!" Wait… How did he know I was looking at a prison sentence? Believing the report of the prophet, I prospered in that word and was exonerated. Now, that's not to say that believing in the prophet alone, exonerated me. Put a pin right there. Omar at least took care of the financial bargaining power with State officials on my end, which helped a great deal. However, later, Omar was arrested again for non-related charges, never to be heard or seen from again.

This is one of the several accounts of God's grace and mercy toward me. I tell you me (in my SFL twang) it wasn't easy picking up the pieces and starting over, BUT GOD! I decided to **Love** again, embrace my **Power**, and **Respect** myself!

I am a Black Diamond. Extreme pressure got me to finally muster up the courage to draw the line. I decided to embrace the worth that others saw in me until I was able to embrace it for myself. You see, I know what it's like to be called a failure by a father who loved and nurtured you but became disappointed when your choices took you outside of purpose. I know what it's like to marry your abuser—you see, I've experienced "deep throat", choked, and thrown to the floor. Sedating myself, only to escape the pain that I would toil in again and again. I know what it's like to fake orgasms, while anticipating his climax and disregard for how you feel. I know what it's like to be called a bitch… whore… even as the wife! I know what it's like to be cheated on… lied to… and served pipe dreams. I've lost friends and family after saying I'd had enough of the abuse and wasn't going back. I know what it's like to be abandoned and treated as an outcast by your very own children. I know what it's like to be swindled out of your inheritance -- by church folks -- rejected by clergy and mentors. I get it; I've been rejected and dejected by those who were in charge of disciplining me.

I know what it's like to be hungry, as a teacher, even as a doctor. I know what it's like to face life in prison, out of loyalty to your man, although he slept with your family member and friends. I've been gunned down because of him on a couple of accounts by females who believed he was their man. I've been spit on, bullied, and harassed. I know what it like to have a family member banging on your door, late in the night, trying to get in, and the scream for help. I know what it's like to be abducted by those who are in authority to protect you, yet, to be sexual assaulted… and the cover up. I've seen the psychologist, only to have the prophecy, diagnosis as mentally incompetent. I've been both far and wide, only to experience discrimination on every level possible. I know what it's like to be envied by others, when in essence, you're not having a great day being yourself. Misunderstood, Hated, Shackled, Imprisoned, Drugs, Alcohol...

It all came with the extreme pressure of being the Black Diamond!

"I am a Black Diamond... Beautiful ... Strong one... Man's got my back with a good Education, Independent... And Depend on... no one to give me hand downs... Pursued it and go get it because I had the right plan... Go-getter personality, perfecting things for quality... That's the kind of queen I am in the family... Grateful, Courageous, Strength to make one nervous, but all I'm looking for is someone I can trust."

Perhaps, you too are a Black Diamond, or considered the "Black Sheep" or the "Underdog" in your family. Motherless, fatherless, homeless... from the White house... to the crack house... to the prison house and/or outhouse. You've been overlooked, oppressed, depressed, or just plain ol' pressed. You've been rejected, ostracized, misunderstood, undervalued, unappreciated, used, abused, desolate, and confused, but wait a minute... I have good news! Although you weren't seen as that clear diamond from the start, there is one thing clear and absolutely uniquely stunning if you will: You're rare... priceless... illustrious, whose brilliance exudes her yesterday.

I wrote a book, called *Black Diamond,* which simultaneously became a stage production and song. The story reflects a provocative profile of an ABDUCTION, SEXUAL ASSAULT, and COVER UP by personnel, in an illustrious hotel in Beverly Hills. The convoluted saga became even the more distorted when highly-acclaimed trial attorneys and judges got involved. Several traits were renowned in the character's personal account; LOVE, POWER, and RESPECT. She realized she didn't make a mistake but another decision that nearly cost her her life. Surrendering to God made the difference and the necessary change needed for the lives of others.

I felt the will and the motivation to change when my children were born. I couldn't do it for myself, but once I laid eyes on my first born, my life changed instantly. Therefore, I encourage you to find something or someone outside of yourself to love.

I leave this personal gift of **LOVE, RESPECT,** AND **POWER**…

Love

"Watch what God does, and then you do it, like children who learn proper behaviour from their parents. Mostly what God does is love you. Keep company with Him and learn a life of love. Observe how Christ loved us. His love was not cautious but extravagant. He didn't love in order to get something from us but to give everything of Himself to us. Love like that. Don't allow love to turn into lust, setting off a downhill slide into sexual promiscuity, filthy practices, or bullying greed. Though some tongues just love the taste of gossip, those who follow Jesus have better uses for language than that. Don't talk dirty or silly. That kind of talk doesn't fit our style. Thanksgiving is our dialect. You can be sure that using people or religion or things just for what you can get out of them—the usual variations on idolatry—will get you nowhere, and certainly nowhere near the kingdom of Christ, the kingdom of God.

You groped your way through that murk once, but no longer. You're out in the open now. The bright light of Christ makes your way plain. So no more stumbling around. Get on with it! The good, the right, the true—these are the actions appropriate for daylight hours. Figure out what will please Christ, then do it.

Don't waste your time on useless work, mere busywork, and the barren pursuits of darkness. Expose these things for the sham they are. It's a scandal when people waste their lives on things they must do in the darkness where no one will see. Rip the cover off those frauds and see how attractive they look in the light of Christ. Wake up from your sleep, climb out of your coffins; Christ will show you the light! So watch your step. Use your head. Make the most of every chance you get. These are desperate times!

Don't drink too much wine. That cheapens your life. Drink the Spirit of God, huge draughts of Him. Sing hymns instead of drinking songs! Sing songs from your heart to Christ. Sing praises over everything, any excuse for a song to God the Father in the name of our Master, Jesus Christ." ~ Ephesians 5:1-5, 8-16, 18-20 (MSG)

Power

Stands for...**P**UT **O**N the **W**ARRIORS' **E**XECUTION **R**OUTINELY

Respect

Respect is a lesson that everyone should learn Respect must be given before an expected return Respect is something that's given for free Respect is about us and never about me Respect is the basis on which relationships are founded Respect is the anchor that keeps a person well-grounded Respect builds the character and defines who we are Respect sets the standard and raises the bar Respect is magnanimous and helps to fulfill Respect is the partner that sits with good will Respect is like honey so sweet it's perceived Respect a taste to savor for when it's received.

~Don Wilson

Dr. Lisa Baxter-Fairclough

Dr. M. Lisa Baxter-Fairclough is a wife and mother of five amazing children. Her home base is the beautiful city of Fort Lauderdale, Florida, but she also dwells with her husband in Wales, United Kingdom, and Jamaica. She is the daughter of Elder Joseph and Lillian Baxter. Friends and news media remember Lisa Baxter for her athletic abilities – MVP and Best in the West - an all-Star basketball team. She is the C.E.O. and founder of U Enterprise International Incorporated - "Making the Connection with the U inside of You" - in neighboring countries such as Kenya, United Kingdom, and Philippines. Her efforts reflect a new psychology called "global community", which promotes cultural diversity and a promising leverage as seen in her other companies, Black Diamond Productions, Black Diamonds & Pearls, and Lilies in the Valley. Her passion for "global community" was inspired by the need for a healthier human survival that is embedded in an entangled web of global economic, politics, social, and environmental realities.

She has been instrumental, through collaboration with other leaders, in assisting with developmental, educational, and economical advancements. Most recently, Christian University of Southern Indiana conferred upon her an honorary doctorate of Humane Letters for life, community services, and outstanding achievements and accomplishments. She's a doctoral learner (ABD) at Walden University in the field of Social Psychology, where she developed a deeper passion for social change. Dr. Baxter adopted two schools in East Nairobi, Philippines, and Jamaica. Her dedication to this "new construct" promotes healthier global communities worldwide while building the "U inside of you", one person at a time. Her mission: to reach and teach all people through self-discovery their best life.

She is a prophetess, chaplain, public speaker, entrepreneur, playwright, producer, author, and life learner.

Life after Abuse
Clara Peters

When life knocks you down too many times, you look to your Father for a way out. When He said, "All you have to do is seek me...watch, fight, and pray", you respond with, "Well, I'm not sure, Father, as I don't feel like going on." He continues, "My daughter, you must. There's some work I need you to do. My child, do as I say and I will direct your every walk, your every talk, as there was a purpose in the pain you went through. Now you must let the women know that life after abuse is beautiful. Speak on it, live it, and show it in your actions."

There have been too many times when I wanted to hide under something because I felt like I'd failed my Father by taking the wrong turn. Yet He kept showing me there was a purpose in my pain. To start the journey, I forgave myself for allowing all that I'd allowed to happen to me in my life with my ex-husband.

After being abused for almost two decades, I came out with a fight in my belly. The fight was to encourage and empower other women, to let them know they have a purpose in life and not to let the bondage they are in or coming out of stop them from reaching their full potential. I want these women to know they do have a voice and God wants them to use it.

Telling your story is not easy, but it is healing to yourself and others like you, as many believe there is no life after abuse. Yet when they not only hear my testimony but see me, they receive hope. They receive the courage God wanted them to see so they can conquer, so they can move past the pain and toward destiny.

The journey has not been easy, but it has been worth it. Telling my story frees me to truly be me. As I tell it, I continue to evolve into the woman He wants me to be. Life after abuse is what you make of it, but I promised my Father that when He freed me, I would fall in love with myself and receive all I needed from Him, to walk into this new life of freedom, to live with a voice and not be afraid of life. Well, I had to remove the many faces I'd put on in the past and just be my true authentic self. I keep walking and talking, peeling back each layer one at a time and dissecting each as I go on this journey of being my true self. It was hard, but I saw the purpose in it. As I kept peeling, I started to see more and more of what I would see when others saw me, and that is a woman who had once been beaten, but was now walking in her purpose, helping others to be healed and setting them free from the hurt of another. I had to learn, that when I trusted and believed in God, I could do anything, as He gave me the strength to fight my way out.

Being able to wake up each day and look the enemy in the face was hard. It was tough to act like I cared to go through life each day, feeling not just unloved but not wanted, desired, or respected, not only as the mother of my abuser's children, but also as a person. I thought God was punishing me for something I did, something I had no control over. Then He showed me my life from birth until that point and I saw that I had a purpose. I didn't do anything wrong. It wasn't me; it was them.

When you have been giving your all to someone and you had nothing left for you, you do wonder: What am I here for? What's my purpose? What's my destiny? Where is my life? I don't want to be remembered as the woman who was abused all her life. I prayed, *Lord, help me help myself.*

Can you imagine being afraid of going to sleep because you don't know if your abuser is going to try doing something crazy to you in your sleep? I was always with my guard up because I never knew when he was going to try me. The life of abuse was daily in some form.

Since finding my voice in 2004, I've made a vow to not just free myself, but to accept what my Father wanted me to do, and that was to also help other women walk into being free to love themselves and know that their lives matter as well. I was seeking love, which caused me to have a life of hell. What I didn't know was I first needed to love myself, then that which was for me was sure to come. Despite the heartache and pain of the abuse, I gave birth to three children who grew to be two beautiful women and one handsome man and who have given me, to date, five beautiful grandchildren.

Yes, the struggle is real, and as I looked at the deck of cards I was dealt, I said, "This is not my hand. Let me reshuffle so I can walk into the hand that was dealt me before birth." God said, "You may be shy, you may be private, but I need you to speak up and out on domestic abuse. You make get nasty feedback but just remember to keep walking with your head held high and a smile on your face, as I will always be with you." God told me, "I need you to surrender and say yes to being that VOICE for the VOICELESS as you birth the ministry that I put in you. Know that you can do and it will be according to what I say. Just listen to my voice and know I will guide you every step of the way."

It was frightening, as I did not want people to really see me. I felt ugly for allowing someone to use me the way my ex-husband did for all those years, yet once God said it was time to release that off my shoulders and let it fall where it was, I started to become, as I aligned myself with Him and the purpose set forth for my life. I asked one of my best friends how I got there, and she said, "I saw it and you cannot turn back." I so did not want that, but I knew I had to keep it moving and let Women of Divine Distinction (W.O.D.D.) be birthed. God said, "That is your ministry name and you will be about EMPOWERING and ENCOURAGING women to be all that they can be. Let them know that they have a voice. Let each woman know that failure is not an option." I kept trying to sabotage it, but He said, "You will not abandon your assignment. You will keep going no matter how hard it may get, no matter how hard it may seem. And yes, you will be walking alone most of the time. Just know that I am always right there."

God gave me 2 Corinthians 3:12-18. "Therefore, since we have such a hope, we are very bold. We are not like Moses, who would put a veil over his face to prevent the Israelites from seeing the end of what was passing away. But their minds were made dull, for to this day the same veil remains when the old covenant is read. It has not been removed, because only in Christ is it taken away. Even to this day when Moses is read, a veil covers their hearts. But whenever anyone turns to the Lord, the veil is taken away. Now the Lord is the Spirit, and where the Spirit of the Lord is, there is freedom. And we all, who with unveiled faces contemplate, are being transformed into His image with ever-increasing glory, which comes from the Lord, who is the Spirit." I was to tell the Women of God to go after their freedom as stated in verse 17 and be that mighty WOG they were designed to be, to stop sitting quietly as life passes by, to get up and claim God's blessing over their lives.

Being you according to God is a wonderful feeling. The weight was lifted from my shoulders, and I was able to truly live. It took me forty years, but I thank God that I am able to live. I have my voice, and I have my wings now. The world is mine as I do the work of my Father.

What am I doing now? I'm living life to the fullest, loving like I never loved before. I am laughing as if it is my last breath and enjoying being the woman my Father designed me to be.

I am a VOICE for the VOICELESS. I am a WOMAN WARRIOR on the FRONTLINE.

Clara Peters

Clara Peters is a pastor, mother of three, grandmother of six, radio talk show host, motivational speaker, mentor, certified life coach, certified peer recovery coach, author, and blogger. She is the founder of Clara L. Peters Ministries and the founder of Divine Distinction Ministry. She is also the founder of the Divine Diva Book Club and the host of Women of Divine Distinction Blog talk radio show.

You can find her on Facebook at:

www.facebook.com/purposeadvisor
www.facebook.com/woddprayer
www.facebook.com/woddbtrs

You can also reach her at:

www.blogtalkradio.com/clarapeters
www.womenofdivinedistinction.com (blog)

If you would like to be a part of the Divine Diva Book Club, send Clara a PM on Facebook.

Empty Sounds
Nolia Rembert

Sometimes I don't have the patience I need with my children. Sometimes I take on the cares of the world. Other times I expect things to go my way. When I feel like I don't have the time, I stubbornly start to realize it is not my time, but God's time. He is the head of my life. It is through the realization of the spirit of God that I am able to submit and be humble enough to say, "Yes, Lord. Yes, to Your will, and yes, to Your ways." His way is the way to being patient and having the love we need in order not to let everyday situations get the best of us. Believe me, it isn't easy all the time, but it is peaceful.

God has allowed me, a "newcomer", to be honest about myself and testify about the goodness of God and how He can deliver us through His Son, Jesus Christ, who has delivered me. This chapter is specifically for people who are struggling to be clean and sober, to help them live their lives right when they really don't know how or where to start.

There's no way you can do it by yourself. Romans 10:9 says if you confess with your mouth the Lord Jesus and believe in your heart that God has raised Him from the dead, you will be saved. Matthew 6:33 says to seek first the Kingdom of God and His righteousness, then all these things shall be added unto you, meaning He will fulfill all your riches and teach you how to live and give you the tools you need to live. God is calling you out of a world of sin and He will show you how to live your life the right way.

I am a forty-year-old woman who has lived over twenty years in the rough streets of Oakland, California, as a single parent, on every kind of drug you can think of, beginning with weed and ending with heroin and crack. I prostituted with women as well as men to support my habit. I was very criminally-minded also, going inside stores and stealing things just to sell them so I could support my drug addiction. During that time, my children were from pillow to post, as my mother would say. They went back and forth from one grandmother's house to another. And did I care? NO!

Eventually I ended up losing my children to Child Protective Services. That is only a short statement of the terror I had to experience when I was living in a world of darkness. I thank God He cared about me when I didn't care about myself. When I think about how I walked inside my house after CPS came and took my children away from me, it makes me want to cry again. I hope no one ever has to experience the empty sounds and the pain I had to experience when I walked through the front door of my empty house. All the sounds of my children crying, "Momma, Momma, Momma!" were gone. They had disappeared, and right then and there, I realized that a house is not a home when you're on drugs and lost in a world of sin.

I remember the tears flowing and flowing from my eyes. They wouldn't stop. You would think that the horror I had just experienced would have made me throw away the crack pipe and cocaine I'd come in the house with, but it didn't. It made me pull on the glass pipe harder so I wouldn't have to remember or feel what I was going through at that time in my life. Not knowing how to pray, not knowing at that time that God was my present help while I was in trouble, I began to holler out to Him to help me.

Those screams were the beginning of my crying out for help, because at the time, I didn't know which way I was going or even how I was going to get there. The only thing I knew was that I was lost in a world of sin and I had lost my kids. I didn't have any hope and I sure didn't want to look at myself in the mirror because I was already feeling ugly and worthless. Satan does come to steal, kill, and destroy. He stole my joy when he stole my children and then he killed my spirit.

First he had me cut all my hair off my head like a boy so I wouldn't have to worry about combing it because I really didn't have time to comb my hair when waking up sick in the mornings for heroin. Then I would go and stand by the fast food restaurants, ashamed and embarrassed, begging for money, lying and saying that I was hungry. Sometimes I was hungry, thinking I might really buy something to eat this time, only to get enough money to go and cop again, only to return back to my begging-and-lying mode.

I remember those times as the emptiest times of my life. I tried going into recovery to find out it does work, only to crumble again, which happens when you don't have Jesus Christ as your Lord and Savior. The first couple of times I went into recovery I didn't have Jesus because I was not ready to give up my old ways or my past. All I wanted was to get clean and sober, get my kids back, and get CPS out of my life so I could do what I do best, and that was get high.

The devil had me deceived into thinking that getting high was good. The devil tricked me into thinking I needed these drugs every day to survive and that I wouldn't be able to function or live without them.

But the devil is a liar. I have never been so happy and content in my life, now that I have Jesus as my foundation. I can finally see things about me that I couldn't see when my mind was clouded from the world of darkness.

My ex-landlord, Mr. Washington was able to see things inside of me I couldn't see myself. Then there was Inger Ackings, a CPS worker who always encouraged me and told me how I was such a good mother and how smart I was. I did not want to believe her. I really wanted her gone so I could get loaded all over again. I did not know at that time I was covering up a lot of pain, which I had accumulated from the time I was a little girl. I was often left alone, only to be fondled by my uncles, my mother, and my brothers. I was always scared to tell because I thought I might get a whipping.

As I grew, my mom left me and my siblings in the house by ourselves daily, sometimes two to three days straight, with strict orders not to open the door for anyone. The only time we were to answer the phone was when it rang three times and stopped, then rang one time. Then we knew it was my mom. So every time the phone rang, we all got quiet and stopped doing whatever we were doing to acknowledge my mom's call. She had us scared to death even when she wasn't there. That is why I thought it was okay to leave my kids by themselves. That is what I was taught. And child abuse... I never knew it existed until I got older and had kids of my own. As a child I got beaten with sticks, extension cords, and water hoses. Once I had my head pushed down inside a toilet and almost drowned because I didn't clean it right. Affection was never shown. You never heard anyone in my house say, "I love you," and people dared you to hug them. My mother also left her boyfriends in the house with me and my sister, who is one year older than me, and they would have sex with us, unbeknownst to my mom - or did she know?

By that time, I guess my mother started coming in off the streets because her girls were becoming teenagers. She started letting us have company and boyfriends, and they were able to spend the night with us. By the age of fourteen I was already pregnant and I had been in juvenile hall several times. I smoked cigarettes and weed and was living on the streets of Oakland on my own, not knowing too much about the snakes and vipers in the world. I was young bait for a lot of old men. They gave me money for sex and told me I was pretty; some even lied and told me they weren't married and that they wanted to marry me.

All this kept me searching for something I did not even know, from one man to another, until I ran into the one who put the first needle in my arm. It was crank. By the time I met my husband at the age of sixteen, I had already been shooting dope only to find out he shot dope too, except he was shooting cocaine and heroin. By the time I had my first son, I was eighteen and married -- a marriage that ended in divorce. He had told me I needed to try cocaine and leave that crank alone and he was right. I'll never forget that first hit I wish I never would have taken. That drove me right where the devil wanted me to be: in hell, but not eternally.

God led me to an outpatient drug program. From there I went to a live-in program. I started to pray the very next morning. I got down on my knees and mumbled all my problems to God, and He heard every cry. God began to deliver me. He helped me to understand who He truly was in my life and let me know only He is able to give me life in a dying world. Ever since God saw fit to save me, I've been running for Christ and I am nowhere near tired yet. I got all my children back and even my grandchildren. God even gave me a wonderful husband.

Now, I'm an outreach minister. I go out and feed and minister the Word of God to my brothers and sisters who are still suffering. I'm also a spiritual counselor and am now attending school to get my A.A. for Substance Abuse counseling. Now with four years and three months of being clean and sober, I can give back what was so freely given to me: grace and mercy.

I have found power in my daily life by doing these simple things.

1. I pray daily to God.

2. I participate in mentoring and coaching programs.

3. I write constantly to help heal my mind, body, and spirit.

God is able to do all things for us that we cannot do for ourselves. He even allows us to hear empty sounds so that we may rest and find peace in Him where our life is no longer empty but full, full of grace, mercy, love, and a sound mind. I will bless the Lord at all times; His praise shall continually be in my mouth.

God can and will do the same for you because God loves you the same as He loves me. You have to be willing or either hearing empty sounds that only God will be able to restore.

Nolia Rembert

Nolia Rembert was born in New Orleans, LA. She has six children, six grandchildren, and is expecting to become a great-grandmother. She is a spiritual writer who loves her work. She is an inspirational speaker as well as a retired substance abuse counselor. It was in 1999 when her calling came, right after losing her children to the state. She entered a drug program, received Jesus Christ as her Lord and Savior, and the newness was in the making. She started the healing process, got her children back, and is still to this day being made whole. She joined a church in Oakland, California, with Pastor Phillip Tinsley, a nondenominational church, and it was there she became an evangelist. She goes out in the neighborhoods and ministers to the lost with food and the Word of Christ. She joined with the now-deceased Pastor Jack in Oakland Midnight Ministries, where ministries still consist of evangelizing.

Nolia obtained an Associate's degree in Human Services. She studied child care and psychology and earned a degree with AACC (American Associates for Christian Counseling), where she studied spiritual counseling. She has numerous certificates to help her live her life and teach women all over that Jesus Christ is Lord and how to live accordingly.

A Once-Hidden Warrior
Samantha Michel

You will again have compassion on us; you will tread our sins underfoot and hurl all our iniquities into the depths of the sea. ~ **Micah 7:19 (NIV)**

November 4, 2008

I remember the Presidential Election Day in which Barack Obama, a man of African heritage, became president. I remember hearing the roar of excitement from the world outside when Obama won against all expectations. It was a miraculous moment. I was in my room, on my knees, praying so hard because, much like America, I needed a major change. I was crying, praising God, and asking Him for forgiveness. I had been a bad girl in the past. I'd had some bad things happen to me in the past. But that was a night for miracles. That night, in a pivotal moment, I knew God cared enough to accept me as His own. God made a change in me. He breathed new life into my weary soul.

I was molested when I was a little girl.

I have heard other women say the same thing: that they were touched, tortured, abused, raped, and spoiled. After being hurt like that, women seem to go in one of two directions. They reject touch and have trouble connecting with men, even if they secretly want intimacy, or they become extremely needy for acceptance from others. They turn into sensual, sexual creatures, and most transition into people-pleasers who need to be accepted: strippers, prostitutes, and women who can't seem to say no.

After my experience of molestation, I eventually grew up and, as a teenager, inherited that spirit of sensuality. I needed someone to want me, but my foundation was in the church. I'd attended church with my parents every single Sunday, along with attending Bible studies during the week, but it wasn't enough. Maybe the church could have helped me if I hadn't felt disconnected. My parents were Haitian and I was first-generation American attending a Creole church that catered to people from the islands. I barely understood the Creole sermons and services. As a young adult of seventeen, I didn't consider going to another kind of church that spoke English. Instead, I wandered away, looking to "find myself". I tried to balance myself and find my identity.

"Who am I?" I'd wonder. After all, I knew God. I knew the ways of the church because I'd been raised in that environment, however, it wasn't a fulfilling life, standing on the outskirts of God's sanctuary. I longed for peace and acceptance. I wanted to escape my feelings and fears. I ran into the arms of men to get those needs met. I tried unsuccessfully living in both worlds, one foot in and one foot out, but that didn't work. The guilt and shame of being sexually active, when I knew it was wrong, made me leave the church scene for years.

As a young adult, I had never dealt with my history of sexual abuse. There are certain mental challenges that come with trying to bury memories and feelings so deep. I was open to corruption and, I confess, I almost lost my identity. I had such low self-esteem that I was an introvert. I went unnoticed because I shrank into the background and I thought I wasn't pretty enough to get attention. I felt I was odd, and as a result, I had to go the extra mile to be noticed.

Relationships in Sin

Being exposed to sexuality at such a young age caused me to be poisoned. The toxin killed my innocence and stained my spirit so that I knew the power of sex. My adolescent eyes became jaded. I was a seductress in a child's body and I didn't have enough knowledge, at the time, to bind that spirit, then set it loose. That spirit of sexuality and seduction took ahold of me. I got addicted to the fast life and getting fast money, and I got involved in adult entertainment (more on that story later in my next book).

Relationships were a major problem for me, especially when I was younger. I didn't flirt much because I was introverted, so when someone paid attention to me, I got caught up and was immediately infatuated. Men know when they can do extreme things to you and get away with it, so I was often a victim. Men knew they could take advantage. When a nice guy finally came along, I didn't know how to deal with him. It's important to know that when we love ourselves, we look better and feel better. We are confident and attract positive people in our lives. It's important to find an identity, especially as a woman, and walk with a posture of a lady, of greatness, which is what we were designed for.

Eventually, I lost what little innocence I had left. I fell away from my foundation in the church and wholeheartedly gave in to the sin of sexuality. They say it's a dog-eat-dog world out there and I have experienced that. After years of chasing money and only feeling validation when a man wanted me sexually, I realized I had to turn from my wicked ways. I would never be a mature human being until I escaped my own sinful existence.

Sin Almost Cost Me My Life

One night I was out with the crew and I received a call. I was supposed to perform with one of the three young ladies I was hanging out with. We were being chauffeured around by a driver. This call was supposed to be for me, I'd been requested by name, but I told my boss no. I told him I didn't feel well and I'd rather not go. I wasn't sick exactly. It was just something inside me, intuition. I felt uneasy and heard a voice tell me something was going to go wrong. I didn't hesitate to listen to this inner voice. I told the owner I was going to pass, even after he insisted it was good money.

I really wanted to go home, but they didn't have time to drop me off, so I rode with the other three girls in the car, along with the driver and the co-owner, to this call. Afterward, the co-owner and driver would take us home. I remember waiting impatiently outside the building in the complex. It was approximately 3:00 in the morning and I still had that uneasy feeling, so I was holding pepper spray in my hand. After about a half hour, I saw a man, dressed in all-black, run toward the back of the complex. I asked one of the girls, who was sitting alongside of me in the car, if she had seen it, but she hadn't. She tried to reassure me everything was fine.

But things weren't fine at all. She didn't believe me until we noticed a lot more time was passing than normal. The driver agreed and got out of the car to see what was going on. He banged at the door to the apartment our girl had gone into. No one opened the door.

The driver got mad and decided to go peek through the window. Lo and behold, he saw they were holding her captive while several men raped her. The driver started yelling, "LET HER OUT!" but they ignored him while they continued to have their way with her. The driver kept banging on the door and threatening the suspects for a good fifteen minutes. Finally, the door opened and the men threw her out. She was naked and crying hysterically. The driver tried to help her up off the ground, but she curled up into a ball and continued to cry. It was obvious she was in a world of hurt.

I remember feeling a guilty sense of relief that I had not gone into that place. I thought, *Wow, that could've been me!* When she was finally helped back to the car, we gave her some clothes. She told us, as she put the clothes on, how they had gang-raped her and emptied her purse.

She kept crying so hard that the co-owner of the operation, who had been brooding silently in the passenger seat, jumped out of the car in a rage. He carried two guns that we girls didn't even know were in the car. He hurried over to the door and pounded on it. I prayed those men wouldn't open the door because I knew the boss was ready to go on a shooting rampage. He held one gun in each hand and started calling out insults to the suspects. When they yelled back, he didn't back down.

At that point, I was breaking out in a sweat. My nerves were frayed and I was beyond scared, wondering if we were all going to die. I remember telling one of the girls, "Watch! We're going to make the 7 o'clock news!" Then I thought, *They're going to wonder what went down. Maybe we'll also be on* First 48, *a local television show where they try to solve murder cases.*

Thankfully, those rapists had the good sense to keep the door locked and barricaded, and eventually, the co-owner was calmed down by the driver. We drove away before the police were called to the scene.

Changing Requires Devotion

The voice inside and that uneasy feeling of wrongness SAVED me! I had been living with one of the girls who was in the car that night. We got home around 5:00 in the morning and couldn't sleep that whole day. Instead, we spent that time thanking God for sparing our lives. That day, God made a change inside me, and I decided to devote myself to Him wholeheartedly. From that night on, I totally changed my life. I made the Lord God my guide and accepted Christ as my true Savior, and I haven't look backwards since. That lifestyle had perks: good money, attention that made me feel sexy and desired, and a family of girls who were just like me, broken inside and needing validation. But getting attention and money for my sexuality wasn't worth my life. I believe there are more important things.

So that day, November 4, 2008, the miraculous day Barack Obama was elected president, God breathed new life into me and I embraced the new identity He gave me. God wants me to be a voice to those lost souls who are held captive to sin. I am meant to be a voice to help free people from bondage.

I know life can be difficult. You can feel disconnected and lost due to shame, pain, and captivity of the mind. There are so many kinds of pain and trauma. Psychologically unhealthy people don't realize you do NOT have to be afraid of living pain-free. You are a person of worth and you don't have to be a victim.

My advice to you is to know that you are important! There is someone who cares out there. No matter what you've done or how guilty you feel, know that everyone has sinned and turned away from God's plan. Find the door of freedom. It is waiting for you to walk out of iniquity and grab the keys of peace, love, hope, and faith. You will experience freedom and self-love in Christ Jesus. Know that you can change your life.

If you are in need, go get help at your local resource center. If you are in danger, go to the police to find help. For those who are local here in South Florida, don't hesitate to reach out. YOU DON'T HAVE TO SUFFER IN SILENCE ANYMORE!

There are many organizations out there that are willing to lend a hand for a person in need. Here are a few resources to contact for Help!

A. Safe Pace shelter - Domestic violence and sexual assault shelter: 305-758-2546

B. The Lodge - Domestic violence, rape and sexual assault shelter: 305-693-1170

C. Switchboard of Miami - Crisis and suicide prevention: 305- 358-4357

D. Roxcy Bolton Rape treatment center - rape and sexual assault hotline: 305-585-7273

E. Miami-Dade County Coordinated victims' assistance center: (CVAC) 305-285-5900

F. Kristi House - sex trafficking hotline 1-877-465-3916

G. Florida Freedom Partnership- Human trafficking hotline: 1-888-373-7888

Samantha Michel

Samantha Michel is a leader who mentors young girls and young adult women through vulnerability and tough life challenges. She is a strong, passionate individual who makes thing happen when she puts her mind into it. She uplifts others with her natural wisdom in every way she can. She is also a humanitarian who travels the globe. One of her experiences traveling was to Africa, where she mentored and helped less-fortunate families and young girls and young adult women who faced poverty, poor hygiene, molestation, etc. Today Samantha partners with campaigns in Africa, where she is one of the campaigns advisors in that country alongside government officials. She is an advocate against human trafficking.

Samantha Michel is the third of seven children. She was raised in Miami, Florida, where she still resides. She is passionate about helping young girls and young adults because of her life experiences. She has a non-profit organization called A Well of Life Changes Help•Prevention•Safety.

Step Out on Faith and Rock Your Season of Victory
Caramel Fairley

Everyone faces a battle at some time in their life. Some battles we fight and win and some we lose. In Exodus 14:14, Moses says, "*The LORD will fight for you; you need only to be still.*" I learned this lesson the hard way.

Two years ago, after a series of trials and tribulations, I felt I was cursed to lose every battle that came my way. I wanted everything handled right away, so why not just do it myself? Why wait on God, since He was busy with more important things? What I didn't realize is that I was trying to fight alone instead of being still and allowing God to do His job.

I began to feel really sick in September of 2014. It was nothing I could explain at the time; I was just "sick". My whole body was hurting from head to toe. Every day seemed like endless muscle spasms, cramping, headaches, inflammation, and dizziness. I went from living to just existing, in constant pain. I decided it was time to tackle this sickness and get some help from doctors and specialists. Sometimes I had to travel over an hour just to see a good physician, but I got up and did what anyone wanted to do if they needed to heal. After many trips to several doctors and failed diagnosis after diagnosis, I slipped into a deep depression. I believed in God and prayed for total healing, so where was He? Why wasn't He helping me when I needed Him the most? Everyone tells you to hold on and pray, but it wasn't working for me this time. Perhaps it was because I had lost my faith. I guess I didn't believe He would heal me anyway. After all, I did believe I was cursed.

I was in so much pain and I wallowed in self-pity and negativity for months. I lost my job. I was faced with foreclosure on my home and repossession of my car. I worried day and night and shed many tears. Instead of using my faith to build me up, I slipped further into darkness. I couldn't eat. I couldn't sleep. I found comfort lying in bed, which had now begun to feel like my own personal prison. My mother reminded me that these were only material possessions, and that if I lost them, they could be replaced. She encouraged me to start focusing on my health and my two sons, who depended on me as their sole provider. I was told "God will work it out" many times. Somehow these words did not provide the comfort I had experienced many times before. Had I actually given up on my belief that total healing would come? Had I given up on me?

One day as I lay in bed, I saw an advertisement for a Joyce Meyer devotional book, *The Power of Being Thankful*. I immediately felt such a strong spiritual connection to the words being spoken about this book. I decided to order it and I had the book in-hand within a week. My transformation began. I started to pray and seek God's total healing. I began to thank God for every day I woke up, even if I was in pain, because after all, I did wake up! My bad days started to get better. Romans 12:12 says, *"Be joyful in hope, patient in affliction, faithful in prayer."* With a positive mindset, I was finally ready to conquer this disease and get my life back. I was learning to exercise patience and my hope for a better future was in sight. I finally began to realize that everything has to work a certain way in God's time, not mine. I continued reading my devotional and praying.

I was soon led to a doctor who actually seemed to care and who wanted me healed just as much as I wanted to be healed. He ordered many tests and checked things that no other doctor had ever bothered to check before. I always complained about all the tests, but after months of traveling to out of town appointments to see specialists, I was diagnosed with lupus. I was ecstatic. Why was I so happy when I'd received such terrible news? "It" finally had a name. Lupus. But what exactly was lupus? I had a friend who had suffered with this disease for years, but I'd never taken the time to ask her any questions. After all, I didn't have the disease. Now being face-to-face with this monster, I had to begin my own research.

So what is lupus? Lupus is a chronic, autoimmune disease that can damage any part of the body (skin, joints, and/or organs inside the body). With lupus, something goes wrong with your immune system, which is the part of the body that fights off viruses, bacteria, and germs ("foreign invaders" like the flu). Normally, our immune system produces proteins called antibodies that protect the body from these invaders. Autoimmune means your immune system cannot tell the difference between these foreign invaders and your body's healthy tissues ("auto" means "self") and creates auto antibodies that attack and destroy healthy tissue. These auto antibodies cause inflammation, pain, and damage in various parts of the body. (www.lupus.org)

Armed with this new knowledge, I could finally begin to prepare my body for any future battles that came my way. Because the lupus was mainly attacking my liver, I stayed swollen and in pain for weeks at a time. I had many trips to the emergency room during these flare-ups. Each time I was prescribed steroids and pain medication, but I seemed to get worse instead of better. What was happening here? I was praying and trusting and believing in total healing, yet my health was continuing to decline.

My rheumatologist suggested I start a healthy eating program to help prepare my body to fight off my current flare-up and any future attacks. It wasn't easy at first. After all, food and lying in bed were my two most-treasured things. I had a lot of support from family and friends. This motivated me to want to be a better person. I wanted to live a somewhat-normal life again.

Almost a year after my diagnosis, I am on a medication that is maintaining my healthy immune system, I've lost sixty pounds, and I was able to return to work after seven months of physical pain and mental torment.

Today my lupus shows no signs of major activity and my body is stronger and healthier than it's been in years. My best friend motivates me daily to stay on track and seek God daily. I know there will be many more hills to climb and battles to fight. I may win some and lose some, but with God's help, I'll make it through!

I learned to always **LOVE** and value myself through any circumstances that came swinging at me and you can too!

1.   You must understand and love yourself first and see your own value before you can love anyone else.

2.   Knowing that God made you unique and special should produce a self-love so great that your shining light can help heal others.

3.   If you love yourself, others will see God's light shining within you and be inspired to claim their own personal victory.

I gained my **POWER** by knowing that this too shall pass:

1.   I begin each morning with prayer, thanking God for this new day of blessings that lies ahead.

2.   I read a passage in my devotional book or Bible scripture as fuel and motivation to complete my daily assignments.

3.   I exercise to strengthen my body. After all a strong, healthy body and mind go hand in hand.

We also believe in **RESPECT** of ourselves and others. Here are three expert tips on how any relationship should be respected.

1.   Allow the other person to have an opinion. After all, we are individuals.

2.   Speak life into your partner. Share expressions of love daily to lift each other's spirits.

3.   Let each person be themselves. Don't try to change them. Respect each other's differences.

Even though I experienced so much pain and suffered with such strong depression that I thought I was going to fail, I did not give up. Once I began to see worry in my children's eyes, my sons gave me a reason to push on. They needed their mom. At that moment I knew that I needed to step out on faith and into my season of victory!

No problem is too big for God to solve. He knows what you need before you ask. Pray to God, give Him your problems, believe what you ask will be done in Jesus's name. We are Warriors who are ready to ROCK!

Caramel Fairley

Caramel was born in Bogalusa, Louisiana. She attended Converse College in Spartansburg, South Carolina, where she graduated in 1995 with a BA in English. She has two wonderful sons, Daniel and Joshua. Caramel enjoys reading, cooking, and selling Avon products and essential oils.

You can contact Caramel at:

cfairley91@gmail.com

The Darkness Within Battles the Light
Nichole Peters

God blessed me with an extremely strong gift that has been with me since birth. It is the spiritual gift of discernment, in which I can sense and distinguish spirits. I have always been able to appraise a person or situation because of this spiritual sight, and because of this strong talent, the enemy recognized my potential and targeted me from the time I became mature enough to judge right from wrong.

One spirit in particular haunted me for decades and put me through major hell. Every time God wanted to bless me, the evil demon that dwelled in my mind attempted to ruin my life. It whispered in my dreams and turned happy thoughts to nightmares. It tortured me mentally and attempted to break me. It wanted to rule me and only gave me peace when I gave into bad judgement. As a result, I made plenty of bad decisions, like dropping out of college and hanging out with the wrong crowd. This story focuses on what happened after I fell deeply in love with a man controlled by a spirit who wanted to beat GOD out of me so I'd turn towards the darkness…

My Darkest Hour

I was on the phone when the first blow caught me on the side of my head. I didn't have a chance to defend myself. POW…BOOM…BANG… Explosions of pain and pulsing red stars were how the first three licks came down. Then everything went dark.

I was out for Lord only knows how long. When I opened my eyes, my head felt like a ripe cantaloupe that had burst open. The ringing in my inner ear was deafening, like an overenthusiastic emergency alarm that wasn't coming to my rescue. I felt blood running down my forehead as I struggled to sit up on my bed. He was there, studying me as my body lay prone and twisted.

Have you ever had your life flash right before your eyes? I did at that moment. He looked so calm, and that scared me more than anything. I stared in his eyes and thought to myself, *I'M ABOUT TO DIE!* I saw the gleam of an evil presence in his gaze that frightened me so deep down; I felt like hot piss was running down my legs. Lord, have mercy, he wanted to kill me! I tried my best to pull it together. I was still conscious, but I was woozy and losing quite a bit of blood. My heart was racing, and fear was causing me to have chills all over my skin.

"How long have you been there?" My voice was weak, my neck stiff, and I squinted as I touched the swelling over my eye.

"Long enough," he said.

I just nodded, sure now that he'd been standing over me listening to my whole conversation. I knew why he was in such a murderous mood. I had been careless. Stupid. He still had a key, and I had been talking to Eddie about leaving him for good.

My big mouth somehow always seemed to get me in trouble. Theron was a total nut when he didn't get his way, insane when he thought someone was screwing him over, and this time, I was the person unfortunate enough to have disappointed him. His eyes said, "MURDER." I knew I had to fight to stay alive.

It was almost like he could read my mind as I gathered the will to fight, to run, and try to escape. At that very moment, he punched me. He grabbed me by both legs and dragged me out of the bed as he beat me brutally with his free fist on every part of my body he could reach. I kicked, jerked, and screamed at the top of my lungs. His hand covered my mouth. I tried to bite his sweaty palm as I cried out from the pain and fear. As I feared for my life, he sat on my numb legs as he shook his head at my weak attempts to get him off me.

"Don't cry, Nikki. You're never that weak, baby. Remember? You're so strong. You're always telling me you don't need no man...but guess what? You were on the phone with another man. Weren't you?" He leaned in so close I could smell the alcohol on his breath. "WEREN'T YOU?!" he shouted. I nodded frantically. He continued, "You say you don't need a man, but it's me you don't need. You just don't want me. You gonna pay for not wanting me." He smiled and finally got off me.

I immediately started crawling on my hands and knees away from him, heading toward the phone, but I guess I wasn't fast enough. My side began throbbing, then I realized he had kicked me dead in my side. I gasped for air. He kicked me again, this time lower in the kidney. It was at that moment I collapsed. My vision became blurry. I began to cry out to God, Lord help me. Please!

He flipped me on my back, then backhanded me in my face. I tried so hard to put up a fight, to push him away, but I was too damaged, bruised, and just barely clinging to life. I felt like I was about to die. My life began to flash before my eyes. I saw my kids, and the visions of their faces were so clear. I could also see black spots surrounding their faces. If I didn't do something, he was going to kill me. The visions of my children would be the last time I saw them.

"Please, baby! I'm so sorry. I'll live with you forever. I'll do anything, just get me to the hospital!" I begged.

"Shut the hell up, you stupid freak!" He jerked me up by my neck and I whimpered. "I heard you on that phone saying you were about to leave me. You said, 'Give me two weeks.'" His breath smelled sour as he pulled me closer toward his face. "Guess what, Nikki? You will be buried in two weeks." He released my neck, and I fell back down on the carpet.

I lay there, barely moving, as he stripped the bloody nightclothes off my welted chocolate skin with a knife. After cutting off my clothes, he got up, walked over to the bed, and picked up something shiny, covered with blood. I touched my bleeding scalp, dazed. I realized he'd hit me in the head with a GUN!

"Get on your freaking knees and lick it." My eyes followed the dull gleam of the gun as he motioned toward his exposed crotch. I tried to figure out when he'd taken the time to unfasten his pants. "I said, GET UP!"

He grabbed me by my hair, wrapped every string of micro-braids he could around his fist, and yanked me upright. "Make me feel better, baby. You will do just what I tell you to do. You better not stop, or I am going to blow your-freaking-head off. Do you hear me?" He cocked the gun and put it against my head.

At that very moment, my body went from hot to cold, then the steel of the pistol pointed directly at my right temple.

"I knew you didn't love me; talking 'bout leaving me. I'm gonna show you to how to leave somebody, Nikki. Only way you gonna leave me is in a box. Nobody else will ever raise my baby. I will kill you and him first."

I was shaking as my tears began to drown me. I was now mumbling my prayer out loud. "Oh my God! Please save me…I need You right now, Lord! Anybody, I need your help please…please save me…"

"You think getting me off the lease is going to get rid of me? I don't care if you did call the police and told them to make me leave. Until you get a restraining order, you can't evict me."

He pushed my face against his erection. OMG… I reluctantly had to take him in my mouth! I had no choice if I wanted to live at this very moment. He was nasty, dirty, and was up to the devil's no-good tricks. His spirit was full of nothing but evilness, and it seems like for a few years, I'd been sleeping with the devil or his son the demon, especially after hearing those voices laughing in my head, sounding real loud and talking to me like this.

"HEHEHEHE… Enjoying yourself? I told you I was coming to get what's rightfully mine!"

Wow… What? That voice in my head, the nightmarish voice from times best forgotten, had chosen this day to reappear. I hadn't had a breakdown since college. Why was the voice back?

"I delight in watching you suffer, Nikki. You forgot and slipped up on your game, hun. I told you I'd be coming back, like a thief in the night."

I was so confused, hearing the enemy's voice in my head, just laughing. I knew right then that this fight was going to be the turning point in the war that is my life. The Bible says, "Do not fear," but I couldn't help but almost hyperventilate from the pain and the overwhelming terror that this man would beat me to death. That voice was back and all I could do was PRAY and ask Father God to renew my strength enough to get rid of its madness. I needed to get away from the severely-disturbed man who wanted to rape and beat a pregnant woman. He didn't know the meaning of LOVE...

Even your fake, so-called Father God warned you of my presence in the good book, but He obviously forgot you are one the biggest dummies who doesn't know my slick, sure-footed self any better. HE HE HE HE...now blow my son real good for me." *(The rest of this story can read in my book,* A Woman of Love, Power, and Respect.*)*

I needed to be the ultimate Warrior and use my POWER to gain RESPECT! I had to become ready to fight against this abusive man, along with the demon voice within.

This is how the warfare with that spirit all began...

Dreams vs. Nightmares

"Nikki, it's about that time again," the evil voice crooned.

Unlike other thirteen-year-old children, I dreaded the end of the school day. The final bell always signaled the coming of the dark hours. In the dark, the nightmares took over. The voices became real, living creatures that chased me, tried to eat my insides, pushing to get into the outside world, into reality.

The nightmares were getting stronger. That dark, demonic voice had haunted me as long as I could remember, and now it was talking to me in the daylight. I was at school, trembling, staring at the clock on the wall. I listened to it tick-tock as time passed much too quickly, but the clicking of the second hand couldn't outrace the frantic beating of my heart.

When the bell rang, I reluctantly stood up as my classmates raced towards the door. I walked to the bus line slowly, sweating harder than a man working out at the gym. I was exhausted. The nightmares were affecting me at school, at home, hurting me both mentally and physically. I suffered with a never-ending pain and the fear that I would never escape the monsters that spent the night abusing me.

I paid no attention to my friends as we waited for the bus. I was too tired to put on a front and pretend that everything was okay. I could barely talk without crying, and I couldn't tell anyone why. How could you explain to your friends that you were getting mistreated by someone no one but you could see?

What do I do? I thought to myself. *Who can I tell my dark secrets to without them thinking I'm crazy as HELL!*

Every time I thought to tell someone, he was there, the demon voice, the strongest monster. He was an enemy I was forced to fight. Every time I closed my eyes, it was war time. Every day, he said the same things over and over.

"Remember, Nikki girl, I own you!"

Like I'd ever forget the tone of his oil-slick voice.

"I know your deep-down, dark secrets. I control your days and nights, every minute of each day."

I fought his darkness. I ignored his words, but it was hard. I was getting to the point where I was ready to give up. Nothing I did made the voice go away. I wouldn't wish the feeling of helplessness on anybody, not even my worst enemy. Except my worst enemy was the voice inside my head and the fear clutching my heart.

My Spiritual War

My mother, Madear, and my grandmother, Grannie, both sensed I was meant for greatness and encouraged me during those dark days to fight. But in order to do great things, I had to go to WAR… and my battlefield was in my bathtub. I use to love to praise and worship the Lord at an early age. I would be so excited to attend church services to see all the singing, dancing, and crazy worshiping going on. So when I got in the bathtub, every moment from church would replay in my head. I'd roll up my washcloth and use it as a microphone. I'd place the microphone on the side of the tub and turn around to start directing the choir. I'd get so loud that Mamma and Madear would make numerous trips to the door to tell me to tone it down. You couldn't tell me I couldn't sing. After the imaginary choir sang all the songs with me, young Nikki would start preaching. I'd have church in the bathroom, just like I experienced on some Sundays, except for taking up the offering.

The demon voice didn't like my praise sessions.

"Look at you, girl! What you're doing is just pitiful. Finally get a little Word in the church house, and Nikki-baby thinks she can come home and do what they do? Fool! You aren't a part of that church. Church folks don't want you mocking them, acting like you somebody. You ain't WORTH NOTHING! A poor piece of project trash, that's all.

I ignored the voice and sang louder. After a bath, I was tired and I knew I needed Jesus to help me take that spirit down! The dark demon voice invaded my dreams in the middle of the night, while I was sleeping like a newborn baby, defenseless and happy.

"Your friends will always be better than you. Their fathers stay home with them every night, not like yours. Your father don't want you anyways. He goes to church almost every Sunday, but does he think to bring you with him? You have to beg to get noticed by your father. Besides, you ugly, Nikki-baby. You're not light-skinned, your skin is dark, and nobody wants a chocolate girl. Your friends always going to put you on the back burner, because you already ain't nothing. You got to take what you got and just work with it. So get back on your level. Stay chained up in the dark with all your secrets."

All the issues the bully monster brought up made me very self-conscious. The ugly monster went even further, mocking me. **"Peek-a-boo! I see you, and please do remember, I own you too!"**

That spirit sounded enraged, talked so loud and in such a devilish tone, it made me want to SCREAM. This unbelievably grating, awful, fingernail-scraping-chalkboard voice had me tossing and turning and shaking harder than

I'd ever trembled before. I thought waking up from the dream would help, so I swam for consciousness, but my reality was distorted.

Spiritual Nightmares

I opened my eyes to a new nightmare. My room was covered with these black-and-neon-colored snakes, slithering across my floor, climbing up the walls, and sliding over my bed. I kicked them away, the salty sweat falling in my eyes, choking on useless screams. The snakes looked deadly poisonous and they sneered at me. Out of their slit eyes, I saw him, the monster, hissing and laughing at my frantic pulsing heartbeat. Loving my fear.

"You tried to escape me, girl, but you can't run for long. You think you stronger than me? You've decided not to obey me? Fine then... Look at what I brought with me because of your little rebellion."

The snakes started to transform into something more than snakes. The black snakes had tracking on them like a new tire, with tiny dots of a sick lime-green all over. The lime-green snakes had lots of tiny red spots. All the black and green snakes had blue pupils and red horns where ears would be if snakes had external earlobes. The psychedelic demon snakes hissed at me as they all slithered closer to where I was huddled in my bed. I felt their readiness to attack and I sat frozen, silent tears running down my face. I was afraid to cry out because I'd wake Father up. I'd tried to get him and Madear to see the living nightmares before, and it had never happened, so I didn't bother trying. Father would just say, "It was just a dream. Go back to sleep, baby."

Dream or no dream, I was so afraid and tired of this unknown monster that I actually tried to have a conversation with the demon in my head.

Why do you keep bothering me?

"I own you, Nikki-girl," the monster replied, **"and lately you've been acting like I don't even exist. I'm sick and tired of you singing all them fake-butts church songs, and the preaching about being saved and sanctified. You will never experience God in your lifetime. You ain't been**

raised that way! I'm your master, you little beast, and this is only a warning."

Fire seemed to be coming out of all the snakes' mouths instead of the normal ribbon, split tongues.

"Don't make me burn you into ashes, little one."

Then the snakes, the voice, and the burning intensity that was haunting my waking nightmares were all gone. I jumped up, ran into the bathroom, bent over the toilet, and vomited. After heaving over the toilet bowl for a few minutes, I stood up and stared in the mirror.

Frustration started to really kick in then, and I started to question God. *Why me, oh my Lord? Why am I going through so much in this unhappy world? I'm sick of these nightmares and being afraid.* God didn't answer me, so I washed my face over and over again, then reluctantly returned to my room to change my sweat-stained gown. I got back in bed but I couldn't make myself sleep. I couldn't risk the monster, the dark demon voice, coming back. I decided to stay up until it was time to get ready for school. I refused to go through that torture again; the hell with this. Eventually I start to nod off, but I fought sleep so I could avoid the horrible dreams.

It didn't work, because I'd played hard that day and I was really tired. Finally, I gave up and decided to rest. Mere minutes after involuntarily dosing off again, I heard the buzzing of the alarm clock, and it was time for me to get up for school. I was tired and exhausted once again. As I got ready for school, I felt all twisted up inside. With the monster in my head not going away, I couldn't be like other kids. After last night's conversation with the dark demon, I knew he wasn't going to leave me alone. This was really getting to be a serious problem.

Nikki vs. The Enemy

The enemy wanted me to kill myself. He sent nothing but negative waves of suicidal thoughts in my head. He would say, **"God is fake, your family doesn't love you, and life isn't worth living. Why not join me? Come get** the bite of your new life. Don't you see? Even the air listens to my command. You can have everything you want if you just do what I ask of you. Get those pills and swallow them now."

I was tired and was starting to give in. I was thinking about taking my grandmother's pills.

"Yes…" hissed the demonic voice. "You are sooo tired and you are doing the right thing. Think about it, girl… no more pain. You are going to be with us now, your family."

The monster's voice sounded pleased, but I was completely terrified. My heart raced, because I'd never thought about joining the demon until that moment of weakness. I remembered talking to my cousin about death, and she told me if I killed myself, I'd go to hell. Why die if I was going to be tortured by the demons in hell? It got me to wondering why the monster was with me everywhere I went? It couldn't be just my imagination; otherwise, I'd be able to control when he talked to me. Should I try to tell my daddy about it, or should I just kill myself tomorrow like the evil monster wanted? He laughed at that thought and started to threaten me again…

"I will see you tomorrow, Nikki. You don't have to worry about none of this any more… You will finally have your sweet peace. Take those-damn-pills and go with me and end this misery. You already living in hell so you'd better do it! You think this is the scariest moment of your life, girl? This is nothing! So don't you dare forget your mission tomorrow? Do you understand?"

That whole night I had cried out to the Lord, and I said, if you just help me fight this war, I will be on your frontline, helping other people he has done this to. Lord Jesus, I am sick of him!! I prayed that whole entire night.

In class, I drifted off into a deep daydream. I noticed that everything had gotten quiet, and I froze, scared that the demon was taking over again. Then I heard the most soothing voice ever whisper a message in my ear.

"You have to fight and fight hard. Never let anybody take anything from you, nor pump your heart with so much fear that you can't win."

I truly started to believe that maybe I was going to be somebody that the enemy feared. My thoughts had me feeling like **Atonement vs. Survival**!!

Leave me ALONE!!! I screamed in my head.

The monster chuckled. **"You upset, little girl? You feeling bad because I hold all power over you? That's what-the-hell you get for not taking the pills. I told you nobody loves you. No one is going to treat you right. I'll make sure of it! I am your master."**

I moaned.

"Here you are looking sad and stupid. Ha ha ha!"

I shouldn't have been surprised that the hissing and cruel voice of the demonic monster was back when I decided I was ready to go to war. Maybe this is all in my head.

"Look, I am tired and can't deal with this right now. Please, please, just leave me alone…" I don't know why I tried to reason with the monster in my head. He felt joy from trying to drive me insane, so deep down I knew this was an evil principality that needed me to lose my mind so I would betray God's vision for me. It wanted to defeat the Warrior in me and kill my dreams of a better future.

"So many problems, Nikki baby. You shouldn't have ignored my suggestion to end it all," he purred.

Visions of me dead, peacefully lying still, with no troubles or bad thoughts bombarded my mind. He kept talking in my head.

"I don't want you to hurt in this evil world. I don't want to hurt you either. It's just you are so stubborn, always challenging me when I want to help you."

I shook my head, trying to get rid of the visions of death and peace. I reminded myself that he did like to hurt me. He loved to control me. There was the time when he said he was going to hurt me badly, then I fell out of the bathtub. There were countless times where he had frozen my lips and my body to stop me from talking, moving or acting like a teenager. The monster loved to see me frustrated and helpless.

"Well, if you don't want to hurt me, give me some space by never returning to me ever again," I pleaded.

The monster sighed. **"You need me."**

Rage poured inside me, filling me up like a cup about to overflow. "You don't care! You want me to suffer. You are always threatening me when I feel happy; now you're trying to get under my skin and make me feel unloved. All you want to do is control me, so why don't you just do whatever the f*** you want to do!" I'd said this out loud, as if he was in the room. It was a good thing no one was home yet because I'd have a helluva time explaining why I was screaming at the living room walls.

"I'm so sick of you not wanting me to be happy on this earth, so just go ahead and take me with you. You want to control me? Come on then, big bad wolf! I'll show you I ain't scared. You can bring your nasty-ass snakes, your voices, and your fire. I'm not going to run, or end up sleeping in my closet, balled up on the floor like a pathetic loser."

"You are still challenging me." It wasn't a question. The monster sounded frustrated.

"Of course I am!" I stomped my foot. "Ugh, you make me sick! You want me to kill myself? Well, I won't. I want to live! So you might as well try to kill me. Sometimes I'm so numb and scared that I don't feel like I'm living. I'm just breathing to exist, but I refuse to go out without a fight."

"You are a silly, stupid child. A waste of air and space! Yet you still defy me when I can torture your mind and your soul. I can control your body, poison your every thought and destroy your relationships."

"BUT YOU CAN'T CONTROL ME!" I shouted. "YOU'RE GOING TO HAVE TO KILL ME. COME ON! FACE ME. BRING YOUR SNAKES AND YOUR NASTY SON JUDAS. PEEK-A-BOO, MY BEHIND!"

There was silence. A shudder ran though me and I felt my legs collapse beneath me. I felt the tears, heard the sobbing, and felt my body shake as I cried, but I didn't weaken inside.

Our Father, I began inside my head, *Who art in Heaven...*

"Not this again!" the monster snarled as I struggled to recall the prayer I'd learned from my Sunday school teacher so long ago.

"Thy kingdom come. Thy will be done. On earth as it is..." I started to speak out loud.

"You little beast! You pray to a force that doesn't exist. A God Who doesn't hear you. I am here offering you peace and you..."

I tuned him out. "Give us this day our daily bread and forgive us our sins..."

The monster snarled. **"I am not ready for you to die just yet. I told you not to ever disrespect me again, but you continue to do so. I'm going to let you suffer. I'm going to break you and torture your mind until you do MY will."**

"Lead us not into temptation, but deliver us from evil."

"You think you have strength to fight! You think your prayers will help! I'm you MASTER, not the empty idol you choose to drop down on your knees for. I hope you continue to be strong you li'l beast heifer! I will be back and will take pleasure from your fall. You will not resist me again!"

"For thine is the kingdom," I began to recite the last part of the prayer louder, "the power and the GLORY...forever!" I paused, because I could no longer sense the darkness in my mind. The monster was gone, for now.

"Amen." After that powerful prayer I felt the Lord Presence and His Almighty voice.

"FEAR NOT, my Daughter. You are of my soul and my spirit. You are loved and you are cherished. FEAR NOT, for I am your strength. I am your strong-tower in the midst of the storm."

Spiritual Wars Can Be Won!

As a youth, I felt peace in that moment because I'd heard God's voice. Real, comforting peace, unlike anything you could imagine. Immediately after I fought the evil as a child, I still remember hearing my mother, as she came through the front door. I felt protected, and from that point on, I knew God had a plan for me. When my grandmother encouraged me to be strong, I developed my inner Warrior and became determined to spread light to the masses and speak life to many who are battling with spiritual warfare. I became the Warrior Nikki-Woman!

As an adult, I was put in a position in which my life was threatened by someone who supposedly loved me. Ladies, please know that love is not violence! If a man puts his hands on you, leave him and the demon that possessed him to hurt you. I wouldn't be alive today if others hadn't prayed for me to be safe. Prayers are so powerful for the health of our bodies, spirits, and souls. Heal yourself by believing that GOD has us covered in His Almighty Wings. Let His feathers embrace you.

I encourage everyone to read Psalms 35 and 91 daily, and if darkness is raging, read Isaiah 60:1-4. It felt great learning how to fight the darkness through prayer and through God's words! I am not who the enemy says I am or who he wants me to be. I'm more than a conqueror. I am the child of The Great I Am... With God's help, I fear no evil!

The

Breakthrough

Warrior

Foreword: Breakthrough Testimony
Rita L. Taylor

Many women are faced with numerous trials and tribulations that test their commitment and integrity. Life sometimes brings unexpected situations that will make us question our faith. The Bible says, in Romans 8:28, that we are MORE than conquerors. I am convinced there is purpose for us all and there is nothing unplanned that happens in our lives. We are all predestined to be the very best we can be.

Always be confident in your ability to strive! The warrior inside each of us pushes us to look deep inside of ourselves and find the success factor that drives us to continue to be our best. The definition of warrior means to have great vigor and courage; to be dedicated to war. We are women warriors who will remain committed until the end. We are women warriors who will give birth to ideas and creativeness regardless of the adversities we face.

There are many examples of women in the Bible who faced adversity but, in spite of the adversity, they never gave up hope. The woman with the issue of blood is one of the warriors who comes to mind. She spent everything she had to find out that natural sources were not the answer to her problem. As women, when there is no outcome in sight, the warrior inside of us continues to search for an answer. Because of her desire and commitment to be whole, her request was granted. This was a perfect opportunity for this warrior to allow doubt to set in.

What we cannot do is give in to the vices of the enemy and be defeated. We must be vigilant on seeking and obtaining our prize! Women warriors will not give in. We will not settle for mediocrity, but will march forward toward victory. Always know there is a warrior inside you and understand that God has fashioned us to win. Some of you may be faced with untimely situations that may cause you to lose hope, but please remember, a warrior never ever loses hope and she never gives up!

There is another brave woman in the Bible located in the fourth chapter of II Kings. The Shunammite woman honored the man of God and believed and trusted his every word. There came a day that her son became ill and died. As a warrior, it is amazing to note her reaction: She took a mental stance to declare that, "All is well!" Her son was dead, but the warrior inside her raised her belief in the power of healing. So when the prophet asked how things were, she responded, "All is well." What an awesome and encouraging testimony of faith!

Storms will come, life will happen, but the warrior inside you will push you on and your belief in God will allow you to grab hold of the "all is well" mentality. The warrior begins to think bigger than the circumstances or surroundings.

We are women warriors who have been faced with unfavorable situations. We are businesswomen who operate with integrity. We are moms who are dedicated to training our children in the fear and admonition of God. We are sisters who encourage and uplift one another. We are wives who honor our husbands and are committed to our love relationships. We are women who love God and believe we are called for purpose. We believe staying positive allows us to do ALL things through Christ. We are women who embrace our God-given creativeness to succeed and live life to its fullest. We are women who live courageous lives. We are women who embrace our ability to be leaders. We are women warriors full of prayer and humility. The contemporary Christian worship group Casting Crowns penned a song that says, "The only way we take a stand is on our knees with lifted hands." We are women warriors who make lemonade when life hands us lemons! We women warriors make life rock!

Mrs. Rita L. Taylor

I forever remain "UNDER CONSTRUCTION"!

I am convinced that nothing happens under the sun that wasn't ordained by God. We have to travel different routes to accomplish our individual goals of success. Life is uncertain, but one thing is for sure: We are all being shaped and molded to be our intended design, the design that was decided before the beginning of time. I pray that you enjoy traveling with me on my journey as God chisels and creates me to be His creation. We all stand at a crossroad at this time in life. What direction do you choose?

Daddy, You're Hurting Me
Wanda R.W. McKinley

"Wanda, it is time for bed," my mother said from across the room. "Make sure your little sister is also ready for bed."

"Yes ma'am," I replied as I put on my sister's pajamas.

I was seven years old and my sister was five. We had a very comfortable life to the outside world. My parents were married. My father was in the military and my mother was a stay-at-home mom. On that particular night, I dragged my sister to the bathroom so we could brush our teeth before bed.

Our bedroom looked like something out of a magazine. We had canopy beds that were decorated in pink and white. The canopy had material that covered the top part of the canopy in pink and white lace hung from the sides. Our comforters were plush and they were also pink and white. Our room had many stuffed animals neatly placed throughout the room.

My sister and I lay down in our beds like we did every night, but that night would be different.

"Good night, Mommy!" we yelled from our room.

"Good night!" our mother, Stacy, said to us.

Stacy and my father, Tony, were in the living room watching the television. A few hours passed and Stacy went to bed. Tony was not ready for bed so he stayed up. After about an hour, my father went to check on Stacy to see if she was asleep. After checking on Stacy, Tony came to our room. He opened the door and my sister and I were asleep. What took place after that was something no one could have prepared for!

Tony walked over to my bed and stood over me and watched me sleep. He kept looking over to make sure his youngest daughter was still asleep. Somewhere in his mind, just watching me sleep was not enough. He wanted to touch me. Tony pulled back the covers and gradually placed himself on top of my small, sleeping body.

"Daddy, what are you doing?" I asked as I woke up from the pressure of my daddy's body on top of me.

"Baby girl, be quiet before you wake up your mother and sister."

"But, Daddy, you're hurting me!"

"I just want to show you how Daddy loves you."

"Stop, Daddy!"

"Be quiet, baby, and let Daddy feel you."

Just then the bedroom door opened and my mother was standing at the door. "Tony! What-in-the-hell do you think you are doing to our child?"

"Stacy, what are you talking about?" My father adjusted himself, getting off me.

Screaming and crying, Stacy yelled, "Have you lost your-damn-mind?"

"Girl, stop overreacting and go back to bed."

I pulled the covers over my head and began to cry. I wondered what had I done to deserve that. Why were my parents fighting? I wanted them to stop all of the yelling and fighting.

After what seemed like an eternity of screaming, my mother returned to the bedroom and got both of me and my sister out of our beds. She left the house with all three of us only in pajamas in the night air.

Tony went to bed because he knew Stacy would be back. After all, she needed him. She did not work and she had two kids.

Stacy drove to her mother-in-law's house, frantic and upset. My grandmother opened her doors to Stacy and listened to her. You see, Tony was and had been abusing Stacy since the age of fifteen, so Tony's behavior was not surprising to his mother. My mother and my sister and I stayed there for a few days, but just as Tony had predicted, she eventually returned home. The incident was never discussed again.

As time went on, the sexual abuse between my father and me never stopped. He did not care about getting caught because he knew he had Stacy in a situation where she had no other choice but to stay. To try to help me, my grandmother began to get me more and she enrolled me in modeling school. From the modeling came beauty pageants and dance competitions. The family would shower me with gifts and cater to my every need. No one realized the kind of person they were molding.

Stacy finally divorced Tony for the third time when I was twelve. Stacy thought she had saved her daughter.

Stacy moved her children to Dallas, Texas, but instead of only two girls, now there was a new addition: a little boy. She had met a guy named Scott who was seven years younger than her. They worked together at her part-time job. Stacy ended up working two jobs to make ends meet. Scott managed to move in with us and things took a drastic turn for the worse.

One day in my mother's room, Stacy, Scott and I were watching television. My mom and Scott were talking about getting married. In my head, I thought it was too soon.

But what came out of Scott's mouth changed the entire atmosphere. Scott looked at Stacy and said, "I do not want to marry you. I want to marry your daughter, Wanda."

Stacy did not even respond to the comment, but in four months, she married Scott. I knew this was not going to be a good situation for me.

I was now thirteen and an honor student. My mother was never at home because she worked so much. One night she had to work overnight and Scott decided he was going to make me his. Once I put my sister and brother to sleep, Scott called me out of the room to get something for him. He lured me into the bedroom where he raped me repeatedly. I knew I could not yell out because I did not want my sister and brother to witness the abuse, so I lay there in my own blood as my stepfather continued to violate me.

There is so much more to my story. I went through twenty-four years of abuse. I was abused by my biological father, my stepfather, my uncles, my friends, and my ex-husband, but through it all, God was the answer.

I am able to share my story, and by sharing, I hope to help and elevate women. When you love yourself, nothing and no one can stop you from achieving your goals. Loving yourself gives you the strength to make it through whatever comes your way. The love you have for yourself will shine brightly so others can see it and know that you are a force to be reckoned with. There will be days when you have your highs and low. We all have them, but it matters what you do when you feel low. On the days where you feel you have reached a low, pray. Prayer helps. Surround yourself with people who love you and support you. Acknowledge what is making you feel low. Identify the problem and come up with a solution to overcome the situation or the emotion that has a hold on you.

We all experience heartbreaks and disappointments. What makes you a better person is learning from the experience. Do not allow it to take over your thoughts and how you feel. Evaluate the role you played in it and make sure you work on what you as an individual could do to better yourself. We all have things about us we could potentially improve.

Relationships are give and take. Some people say it is 50/50, but I say it is 100/100. Each partner gives 100% of himself or herself. Dedicate yourself to listen and to be patient and understanding. You must be thoughtful and continue to nourish the relationship. Just like a flower that needs good soil and water to grow, so does a flourishing relationship.

Never give up on yourself. Never allow someone to plant negative seeds in your life. Never think something is not achievable and never compare yourself to someone else. God made each and every one of us different. He gave us different gifts, and your outcome and results will not be the same as your neighbor's. Embrace who you are and love your imperfections. We all have them. God did not make us perfect. Know that you and no one else controls your destiny. Even surviving abuse, it does not make you and it does not have to control you. As a survivor, you will never forget what happened, but you can get through it.

God was the answer to my survival. God is the reason why I can write my story as well as talk about it. I pull my strength from Him. I call on His holy name. I can tell you there are good and bad days, the highs and lows, but if when you are at your lowest, call on Him. God will never forsake you and will never leave you. Turn to Him and He will bring you through.

Hear me ROAR.

R - Regain who you are.

O - Overcome the abuse.

A - Achieve your self-esteem.

R – Rebirth yourself as a child of God.

Wanda McKinley

Wanda McKinley has been a part of the Dallas community for thirty years. Her family relocated there from California when her father retired from the Navy. She has been educating families for twenty-two years in the insurance and healthcare industries, believing that knowledge is power. Mrs. McKinley has worked in the Long Term Care Industry for eighteen out of the twenty-two years taking care of the elder population and educating them on the correct way to spend retirement funds as a licensed financial advisor. In November 2013, God showed Mrs. McKinley her purpose in life. God told her, she must be transparent to men, women, and children who have experienced domestic violence by sharing her story so that they would find comfort through her.

Through the grace of God, she survived twenty-four years of abuse. Her calling and passion is to help others. We Are Survivors was formed as a 501(c)3 non-profit organization for abused men, women, and children. Their mission is to provide a stable environment for abused and battered individuals by providing temporary shelter, counseling, and employment training. They want to help them transition from abusive situations to being self-sufficient people in society.

Mrs. McKinley is currently attending University of Phoenix to obtain her Master's degree in Psychology. Understanding the pain on a personal level will help her relate to the men, women, and children God sends to her, but she will also be able to provide professional counseling. Mrs. McKinley is a strong and powerful domestic and international speaker who has also appeared on television and radio talk shows. Believing in God and hearing Him has carried her thus far. She is a child of God and has embraced what he has for her. May God be given all the glory as she continues on her journey

A Young Warrior Never Quits
Shamaine Peters

Even though I technically grew up in the projects, life for me was easier than most, because I was blessed with a mother and father who gave me everything I asked for and more. My grandmother, Ma'Dear, spoiled me too. Our family was big and blessed. My mother was the baby out of her 9 siblings (on her maternal side). She was also the baby of 10 other siblings on her father's side. I never experienced loneliness because I had a ridiculous number of cousins who lived quite close to me. I also had plenty of friends not related to me. I loved growing up with so many children running around in the projects.

I am from a very small town in Louisiana, called Bogalusa, which is located about one hour from New Orleans. I came from a real family who didn't believe in hiding. There were few secrets. We were always willing to help our neighbors and we never hesitated to open up our lives to others. We were a very tightly-bonded group with shared values and rules to follow, but like every other family, we had our share of ups and downs. We occasionally disagreed and had arguments, but we always respected each other and made up.

Carrying Me to Safety

My mother gave birth to me about two and a half months before her due date. There were complications due to her hypertension. She also had a weak cervix. As a result of her heath issues, I and all my siblings were born premature. I remember her explaining to me she'd been very sick when she was carrying me. She'd been forced to go on maternity leave 5 months early. She was constantly in and out the hospital while carrying me.

I found out later that my mother's OB/GYN warned her that having a child would be dangerous for her. Her doctor hinted that, with my mother's severe hypertension and the new development of **gestational diabetes**, it might be better to eliminate the pregnancy. However, Mom refused to abort me. She did not believe in abortions, period.

"Dang, Ma," I said to her when I was in high school. "You went through it! I'm glad you kept me, but it must have been so hard." My mother just smiled and told me all the pain was worth it.

"I knew you were going to be something special," she said. "You better have been special, after putting me though all that pain and stress."

After her water broke early, she was forced into a dry birth that caused her punishing pain and made her blood pressure skyrocket. To this day, we both thank God for sparing both our lives. I also thank God for letting my mom carry me almost six months safely. I often think about this story and I smile because I have never had doubts about my worth. I knew I was valued because my mom could have lost her life giving birth to me. It makes you feel cherished to know someone is willing to risk their life to make sure you live. My mother's story proves that there is true self-sacrificing **LOVE!**

School Dazed

Years went by, and it came time for my mother to register me for kindergarten. As a five-year-old, I was super-excited about going to school. I really loved my teacher and the other kids. I never wanted to leave. I even wanted to go to school on the weekend. My grandmother lived with us at the time. She told me stories about how she used to laugh at me because I cried on Saturday mornings when no one would let me get ready for school. But even though I loved school, some days, school didn't love me. By me being premature, I struggled with certain subjects, even on an elementary school level. And some of the children, who I guess were jealous of my pretty face and the nice clothes my mother dressed me in, were beyond mean.

Some days I'd have to fight back to show the bullies I wasn't afraid of them. I didn't mind standing up to bullies on the behalf of others either. I thought making fun or fighting a person because they looked different, talk different, and believe different things than you do was cowardly. I stood up for myself and others because I watched both my parents stand up for themselves. My parents were respected and well-known around our town as people you didn't mess with. However, people loved being around them. Everyone still tells me to this day stuff like, "Your mom and dad were a crazy, fun couple." I'd laugh and agree. I inherited a strong will as well as a fun-like craziness from them both.

Hurricane Katrina

I was 12 years old on August 29, 2005, which was the first day Hurricane Katrina crashed through Louisiana like a wild woman. The storm had a personality that was vengeful and she took out her anger on so many people's houses, vehicles, streets and businesses. The storm was so mean that hundreds of people were forced to relocate with government help. My mom was one of those people who decided she needed a new start. She decided to relocate to Texas after the storm destroyed half of our possessions. She also made the decision to bring all her children to Texas too. I was spoiled by my big family and I was such a grandma's baby, I couldn't imagine not living near my relatives and pleaded to my mother to please not make me leave. My mother said she planned to move in the summer, a month after I finished 7th grade. I suggested that I stay with Ma'Dear. My mother shook her head no.

"Mainey, you are coming with me. The new house is in an awesome school system that will help you and provide the resources you need to become a better student. We aren't growing here. This move to Texas is a fresh start and new beginning that will help all of us. This move will become our new great beginning."

After hearing her passionate speech, I had to **RESPECT** my mom's decision. She made me believe, and in less than 90 days, I found myself truly loving Texas. I was exposed to new things. Everything was so big and spread out. Where I came from, everything was so small. It took a while to adjust to that part.

Hurricane Katrina was truly a bad storm that caused so many people to lose their lives and their livelihoods. The storm was a cause of great stress and hopelessness. However, it was a blessing in disguise for us. I am glad Mom made a change and used a force of destruction to create a fresh start for us. I experienced blessings in life like never before by transitioning; much-bigger and better-equipped schools helped me to grow and succeed academically for the first time. My life totally changed.

As years passed by, the bulling lessened, but academically, school seemed to grow more difficult for me. My being born premature took a toll on my development and I struggled with deficits because of my neurological nerve disorder, emotional behavioral disorder, and my ADHD. I was also diagnosed with rheumatoid arthritis as an adolescent. Some days it felt like a train had run over my tiny body and dragged me for miles. Every muscle in my body screamed in pain. Some days I could barely move and I missed weeks of school. I was going back-and-forth to the doctors for solutions that didn't help. Some days in class, my muscles would lock up, and I couldn't even hold my pencil or pen because the inflammation was so severe and painful. This worried my parents and grandmother so much. There was a different type of pain that came from watching my favorite cousin and best friend die from cancer.

My grades were dropping because of the stress from being sick, from my best friend being desperately sick, and from missing classes. I fell behind and performed so badly on that year's State testing that school officials wanted me to be tested to see where I was developmentally compared to students my age. After days of being tested to see where my IQ was, my results were troubling. I was more than a year behind my peers when it came to academic knowledge and needed to be held back. The resource teacher told my family I had slower-than-normal processing that most likely had come from being born so early.

I will never forget the look on my mom's face. She was so hurt and blamed herself and her weak cervix. She felt it was her fault because she couldn't carry her babies to full term. She cried and said it was her fault that I was struggling mentally, physically, and socially. But later, she dried her tears and looked me in the eye. She told me the whole family was going to fight to help me succeed and prove all those tests and anyone at that school wrong. She was determined to make sure I was successful no matter what. Everyone else in my family agreed that this diagnosis wasn't going to hold me back. Ma'Dear told me to pray and think like a winner. Daddy told me there was nothing I couldn't accomplish. My mom told me there was a warrior inside me. She told me to hold onto my guts and dig deeper so I could fight and believe in myself and my dreams.

S.M.I.L.E.S.

I guess a few of you are wondering, what is **S.M.I.L.E.S.?** The acronym stands for Sisters Motivated In Literacy (for) Excellent Students. I started the organization with my siblings because we all suffered with certain learning disabilities and neurological challenges. The actual name also honors my late cousin, Parish G. Peters, who passed away from Neuroblastoma cancer in 2011. He told me that no matter what I was going through, always smile and stand tall and strong.

After all my experiences, I knew I needed to help bring more hope to students who think they cannot succeed because of disabilities. My goal is to prove that, no matter how hard it is to do well in school, you shouldn't give up. I want to scream to the masses of students who think they are too-dumb or messed-up to pass a class or graduate and become successful that, "Yes, you can!" A scripture from the good book says, "Anything is possible for those who truly believe."

I believed in S.M.I.L.E.S., and now our organization is growing and helping those who struggle with school clothes, supplies, and assistance with tutoring to help students climb higher. S.M.I.L.E.S. also helps students who have low self-esteem due to bullying. We provide positive reinforcement and self-beauty tips. I often host beauty classes to show girls the best way to get dolled up, one smile at time.

Baby Steps

Not only did I beat all odds and graduate from high school, but I did so in three years. I later became certified to become a pharmacy technician and I worked for Walmart for years. After delivering my beautiful baby girl on September 27, 2015, and I didn't return to Walmart after maturity leave. I instead turned to where my heart was and that was to S.M.I.L.E.S. I decided to take my organization full time and help this nation.

Now that I've contributed to my second anthology, I feel I've overcome a major obstacle. My future goals are in the works too. In 2017, I will have my own television show called *Sending Smiles All Across America*. I'm determined to be a role model to all young warriors and help provide a breakthrough and blessings to others. I know no weapon or wall that tries to stop me will be successful. Please know that, no matter how painful life is, there are ways to grow stronger and live a great life. Consider these tips:

Love

Always love who you are and know who you are. If anyone ever tries to take away from your self-worth, he or she is obviously not good at loving you. Protect your mind, body, and soul. Know that God loves us all and you should love yourself too! As a warrior, you should know you must love in order to become a great fighter!

Power

How you handle power is actually up to your mind and your heart. We gain power from harnessing the gifts God has given us. We must recognize our talents and our strengths, and use that confidence to control any weakness, hopelessness, and negative feeling standing in your way to becoming the strong person you are meant to be.

Respect

Growing up in a poor area taught me that the most important thing isn't how much money you have or how much name-brand material things you own. If you don't have respect that comes from within, it doesn't matter who you are or where you come from. Treat everyone right and show a positive attitude. If you don't agree with a person's opinion, mind your business and leave other people's business alone. I hate bullies and I think that the upmost respect anyone can give is mutual respect to others even if you don't agree with their point of view.

Respect brings Peace, which is Power, and that shows you are aware that Love is **GOD**!!

My Challenge

I challenge every Women Warrior to think outside the box and welcome in light. Receive love, power, and respect, then turn around and give it back. Seek wisdom and understanding. Starting now on this day, and each and every day after that, have faith, smile all over, and work on improving your mind, body, and spirit. Be prepared to execute a plan or goal that will make the devil mad. With your full armor on, battle against any possible failures and fears. Challenge life by believing you too can make it!

I know for a fact that I am destined for greatness, and I'm ready to become a wise warrior because I'm already a young warrior who constantly fights for others just like my mother does. She is a great example of what a warrior should be: a fighter who stands on the front line, who urges others to fight with her. Let's roar, rumble, and ROCK because we are Women Warriors Who Makes It ROCK...

God bless you all!

Shamaine Peters

Shamaine Peters is one of the three founding sisters of the organization S.M.I.L.E.S. Academy (Sisters Motivating In Literacy Excellent Students). She loves to model true confidence by rocking her fashionista diva style in order to help students who have been bullied due to their disabilities. She focuses on helping students with achieving, believing, and rocking an "I can be somebody too" confidence. Her S.M.I.L.E.S. Academy program helps at-risk students who struggle in school by providing them with free counseling, tutoring services, self-esteem-boosting sessions, after-school learning programs, and by offering training services.

After being diagnosed with mental retardation due to IQ testing, Shamaine didn't let this diagnosis define her life. With the help of her supportive grandmother and her never-give-up mother, who wanted nothing more than to see Shamaine and her siblings succeed, Shamaine graduated high school in three years instead of four with a rocking 3.0 GPA. She is now the COO of Women of Love, Power and Respect, and Believe In Your Dreams Publishing. Shamaine's upcoming book, *Your Diagnosis Should Not Stop You; Let It Motivate You Instead*, has a release date set for November 2016, and her future upcoming TV show *Winning Smiles Across America* will be launching in February 2017. She is fast becoming one of the youngest female motivational speakers to gain media attention.

Shamaine was born and raised in Bogalusa, Louisiana. She is the oldest of her three siblings and the loving mother of one beautiful duchess. Shamaine believes that with God on her side, there's nothing she cannot achieve. She brings them an inspirational message: "I am a walking testimony that anything is possible for those who do believe in themselves. Now SMILE...there is hope! You can move mountains if you just simply believe in order to achieve."

www.faceboo.com/luvpowerrespect
www.twiter.com/smilesbeautyamerica
www.motivateurmind@yahoo.com

A Gracious Warrior Who Makes It Rock
Tamatha Robinson-Wilson

Eight Is Enough... remember that show from the 70's and 80's? Well, that was my life as a child. I was raised in the Redmond Heights Projects, apartment #30, in Bogalusa, Louisiana, with a survival mode like no one else I have ever known. Being the eldest of eight children under one roof was very interesting. Being a bossy, rebellious daredevil that feared absolutely nothing or no one was the rule of the game I played. If or when I felt neglected or abused, there were absolutely consequences and repercussions. I needed anger management like a fat kid needs sweets. I would fight a bear and win. Bear with me here; this is my testimony.

Now I give my battles to God and He handles it for me. I was the rebel, the runt, the black sheep who wore it proudly and well. I can recall getting into it with my mom often because of my stubbornness and rejecting her instructions - and anyone else's, for that matter. I was Tammie, and Tammie did what she wanted, when she wanted.

Then I grew up. That strength that refused to be altered endured abuse on all levels. In one relationship I recall being strangled until I could not speak. His hands grasped one side of my face and the other hand was under my neck while he stood behind me. It was something like a horror movie in hindsight, as though he was in the process of breaking my neck. I remember relaxing, because I knew I was about to die and I started to pray like never before, and he let my head and face go. The on-again/off-again relationship came to a screeching halt. I walked away bruised and ripped emotionally, but my spirit was stronger than it had ever been before. At that moment I knew no man, woman, or child would ever break whatever destiny and purpose I had inside of me.

After leaving for the last and final time, I began walking to the mirror and affirming: "You are beautiful inside and out." "If you can see it with your eyes, you can hold it in your hands." "You may have bent, but you are not breakable." "You came from a line of strong women; therefore, you are strong." I often use those affirmations when I sense any form of alteration in my spiritual walk or any relationship that seems to be draining or trying to bend me. Yes, I said bend! We are bendable because we choose to be, but know that no matter what comes or what may be, you are never breakable. You were not built to break!

Life can be a battle or a battlefield. It's all about perception. I choose to look at it as a battlefield. Every day is not a battle, even though we are on a battlefield. We have to assess a situation to determine if it is indeed a battle. If it isn't, we have to move along and not exert unnecessary energy on things we are not meant to fight. We should use our energies fighting for things we believe are right, to fight against injustices, targeting those unable to advocate for themselves, and stand up for what you believe while fighting. Those things made me the warrior I am today and choose to be from this day forward.

Strong women are like palm trees. When life comes in like a storm, they're flexible. They bend (on their knees) like the palm tree during the high winds that refuse to stand tall to endure damage and brokenness. After the storm, the palm bounces back, stronger than ever. It bends, but is not broken.

Never give up! If you're knocked down, pushed down, misused, or abused, never give up! Get up, dust yourself off, and keep it moving. Never allow external things to tamper with or alter your internal peace.

When life brings uncertainties and we are left shaken, bruised, and broken, we can find comfort in knowing God didn't allow us to come to the storm in order to leave us in the storm. Solitude and sunshine is soon to follow. Take shelter in His grace and protection within His loving arms and in time know that this too shall pass.

Always trust your spirit - that quiet voice that NEVER leads you wrong, that voice you wish you would have listened to when you make the statement, "I should have followed my first mind," or "Something told me not to do/say that." Your spirit will guide you if you relax, listen, and obey. Make a plan, execute the plan a little at a time, and stay focused. If you reach your goal a little at a time, it means a lot more than not trying and not reaching your goal. If it isn't encouraging, motivating, or inspiring, it's attempting to break you. See through the façade and stand tall like the woman you are!

Love Tip:

Love, I believe, enhances this journey called life. It's like a bright light that shines in the darkest places. The light of love exposes dark and hidden things. Refuse to be left in the dark.

Learn to love yourself before you can receive or give love to another. Love is embracing what is, accepting what is not, and not force-fitting anything. God is love. If one believes in Him, love soon follows.

Also, when we give love, it returns back greater than we can ever imagine.

Power Tip:

Power is a perception. It flows from the inner part of your being, only as strong as what you are connected to. The electricity in your home uses high voltage to produce the power needed to perform its job. A remote control needs less voltage because its duty requires less. Too much is given, much is required. Power is transformed from a source to you, and the higher the plane or deeper the calling, the more power you will receive. An old cliché holds true: "No prayer, no power; little prayer, little power; much prayer; much power!"

Respect Tip:

Simply put: respect isn't given and it can't be purchased. It has to be earned. It's like a boomerang. If you want it, you give it and you get it back in return. It's a token of appreciation given to those who walk with integrity and stand for what's right.

Love, power, and respect are vital characteristics that simply flow from within and radiate outward to captivate other warriors. They not only bring peace and joy, but they give you the ability to forgive those who spitefully misuse you.

Imagine yourself as a form of currency. People sometimes take and mark your form as worn, torn, or insufficient. Let's use a check for this discussion. Some checks are valuable, but haven't yet been endorsed or signed. Some checks have been marked as insufficient and others stamped with "void" to cancel a transaction. Aren't you glad man doesn't have the power to determine your worth? I am! When the real and only true Accountant deposits worth on you, no matter what your form of currency is, the checks and balances always add up to what He says it should be!

With that being said, don't allow others to determine your worth! You are who God says you are! You are worth what He says you are worth. You are valuable! You are an asset, NOT a liability. Keep striving and the checks-and-balances in your life will and shall be what they were intended to be in the end - if you only believe...

Tamatha Robinson-Wilson

Tamatha is a nurse from Tomball, Texas, by way of Bogalusa, Louisiana. She attended Bogalusa High School and graduated in nursing from North Shore Technical Community College. The stones and trials of life were used to build upon instead of allowing them to break her. Her life's motto is, "Bent, but not broken."

Tamatha is a full-time nurse doing what she was called to do: care for those that are broken physically, spiritually, and emotionally. After working dead-end jobs as a salesclerk, receptionist, and customer service tech, just to name a few, she decided life was calling her to do and help more. She prayed for direction and went to school to become a nurse.

She is the eldest of eight siblings and four half-siblings and the mother of seven beautiful children - three by marriage - and two granddaughters.

The survivor of abuse, she has decided to give back to women who, even though bent, refuse to be broken. Her plans for the future include a safe house to not only shelter but reconstruct these women from the inside out, providing resources to build self-esteem, character, and spiritual stability, and a total makeover. "Bent but not Broken" will be manned by other women who have chosen not to allow life to break them, but transform them by their flexibility to bend but refuse to break.

tammie.robinson1972@gmail.com

A Roaring Warrior Breaking into Her Freedom
Melissa Cadenhead

When I was five years old, my mom had someone who was supposed to be a good friend of the family and her daughter start to babysit me and my brother. While she was watching us, she told my brother to go in the back and she told me to stay. I stayed to watch my favorite cartoon. She went into the back to change into a nightgown and she told me to lay down on the sofa. When I did, she rubbed her private parts in my face. When I moved my face to the right to try not to let my mouth touch anything, I started crying. My brother came in, hit her with a shoe across her back and told her to get off me, and that he was going to tell my mom. She tried to say it was okay, that she was just playing and turn around. I was so afraid to tell because the babysitter was my mom's close friend and I was afraid I might cause a friendship to break up. But finally by the third time, my mom asked me what happened; I broke off in tears and told her. My mom went off, ready to try to fight the lady, but my dad stopped her, and my grandma and my aunties started to keep my brother and me.

I moved to Miami in 1991 and everything seemed to be okay. I made new friends and started going to church and children's Bible study. It seemed like my life was going well until my neighbor's house became a very dark place for me once again in my third-grade year. At the age of nine I was raped by a seventeen-year-old young man. I was so scared to ask for help, and as a nine-year-old, I didn't think anyone was going to believe the word of a child over his. It went on for six months because he kept threatening me and manipulating me into doing whatever he wanted. One night I wet the bed and I called his name out; my sister woke me up, asking me what was wrong. I started crying and I broke down and told her everything. She ran and woke up my dad and mom, and they called the police. The police took me to the hospital and the nurses did a rape kit on me. It was traumatic and it affected me physically, mentally, emotionally, and spiritually for a long time.

In high school, there was a girl named Sandra and she was supposed to be my friend - until she set me up with this young man named Larry. Every girl liked Larry and I was happy he'd picked me out of all the other girls. Larry and

I exchanged numbers and we began to talk for a few months. We would talk in the hallways and on the phone for hours. One night on the phone, he told me to skip class the next day because he wanted to do something special for me. I dressed up in something beautiful the next day and his cousin came in his car to pick us up. When we got to his house, the atmosphere did not feel right at all and I wanted to leave. Larry suggested we go sit in the car, and I agreed. He asked me for a kiss, which I gave him, since he was supposed to be my boyfriend, but then he took it farther and stuck his hand up my skirt. I struggled to get away and told him "no", but he ignored my pleas and forced his way inside me. Then his cousin came to the car and said, "I got next!" and he proceeded to rape me too; then a third person came and did the same thing. I ended up breaking the glass window of the car door with my clog sandals. Larry slapped me and kicked me and told me to find my own way back home. Two guys standing outside – I'll call them Batman and Robin – watched it all happen and did nothing, saying it was none of their business. I thought I was saved by the bell by another young man, who offered me a ride, but his car wouldn't start so a friend of his offered his car instead. They made a stop and the boy in the passenger seat hopped in the backseat with me and he raped me too. I was in a state of shock. The driver pulled him off me and I finally made it home.

The next day at school, Batman and Robin told everyone I'd let a train get run on me. Larry threatened me and warned me not to tell anyone the truth. I allowed people to believe a lie. I was too afraid to tell anyone what had really happened. I began to think God had stopped loving me and was giving up on me, and I felt like everything was going in circles. I still did not feel spiritually free because with every relationship I was in with men, it seemed like I always drew the ones who manipulated me. For some reason I could not keep away from them, but God's strength helped me to stay focused and His strength helps me to stay positive at all times.

Never allow fear to overcome you. If something in your spirit tells you it doesn't feel right, LISTEN. That is God speaking. Do not ignore it. When something negative happens, tell someone so you can get help and advice, and in turn, you can help the next woman. Pass on your experiences and the things you have learned to others so they know they are not alone. I regret not saying anything about my abusers from the start because I was so afraid of what might happen to me, but I needed more faith in God at the time.

You can live a happier, more positive life if you follow these steps:

Love

1.   First and foremost, love God with all your heart.

2.   Love yourself.

3.   Love others the way Christ loves you.

Women should love themselves completely because they are children of God. Each of us has a gift and talents that God blesses us with. We are queens and we should love ourselves as such.

Power

1.   Uplift those around you. There is strength in giving others an emotional or spiritual boost.

2.   Speak positively to the people you encounter in your daily life.

3.   Be encouraging to others and help those who may be struggling, even if that means doing something as simple as lending a friendly ear and just listening.

Respect

1.   Be honest with yourself and with others.

2.   Be humble in spirit.

3.   Stay positive in the face of adversity.

It can be difficult to remain positive sometimes, but I have found that doing these three things can really help you to maintain a good outlook in your daily life:

1.   Do a devotional prayer for thirty minutes.

2.   Read the Bible and motivational books. I do this as part of my morning routine as I sit and drink my coffee to start my day.

3.   Exercise/work out. Keeping yourself in a healthy physical state will help you to stay positive mentally and emotionally as well. I personally listen to uplifting music while I work out to get into a more positive mindset and to stay motivated.

I challenge every Woman Warrior who is reading this to Make It Rock. You have the power within yourself to do anything you set out to accomplish. I challenge you not to give up on yourself, no matter what obstacles you might encounter. I challenge you not to lose hope even when things seem hopeless. I challenge you not to lose faith even when you feel discouraged. I challenge you to believe in yourself and, most of all, to believe in God, no matter what. He is there to cover and protect you every step of the way, without fail. I challenge you to overcome the fear of the enemy and not allow it to control your life. I challenge you to break the chains of all the negative things that have happened to you in the past. Look in the mirror and say to yourself:

"I am a beautiful queen just the way I am!"

"I am a woman warrior who will make it rock!"

"I am breaking into my freedom!"

The main advice I will share with you is that God loves you with all His heart. You do not have to allow fear of the enemy to take over your life because the power of God is with you at all times. Break every chain!

Melissa Cadenhead

Melissa Cadenhead is the Ms. Runway Ambassador 2016 for first class production Miss Runway. In 2015, she took home the title of Ms. Runway First Runner up. She was born in small town Camilla, Georgia, but later moved to Miami with her family. She went to City College and earned two degrees, one in Legal Assisting and one in Broadcasting. Melissa has also received three certificates, one from WMKG TV, one from Cox Radio in Orlando Florida, and the third from the broadcasting club at City College, where she received an outstanding contribution as a secretary for the broadcasting club.

Melissa has been dancing ever since she was twelve years old. She also became one of the fastest runners for the Westview Middle track and cross-country team. At the age of eighteen, she joined a modeling company and learned all about fashion. At twenty-one, Melissa joined Acting like Crazy, where she studied and improved her skills for commercials and TV. Melissa has been in three TV shows (*Burn Notice, CSI Miami, Reno 911*) and two independent films (*Dri and Carmen, Life of the Party*). She has also done three fashion shows.

Melissa has created her own talk show in Atlanta called *The Melissa Star Show*. It is now being seen on twelve different websites. She is also a model/actress/hostess/promoter. Melissa's goals are to build a praise dance company for teenage girls and to have her talk show go far. Most of all, Melissa's goal is to work hard in the entertainment business and put everything inside God's hands.

Rocking My Love Power
Edwanna Smoot

I am a single mother of four wonderful children, my gifts from God - or my "heartbeats", as I often call them. As much as I love my children, I never thought I would have to face the things I have faced with them alone.

My journey started years ago while I was still in high school. I was one of those "good girls", as small town folks would say. I come from a two-parent home, Christian values, and middle class. Can you imagine my parents' faces when I told them I was pregnant at the age of sixteen? After a high-risk pregnancy with my oldest, I still managed to graduate with my class two years later. Fast forward four years and I had my oldest daughter, two more years and I had my youngest daughter, and finally, three more years and I had my youngest son. I did not do this alone, but I got left to handle every trial and tribulation on my own. I had big dreams and was not going to let anything stop me - not even being a single mother. I took my children to church and explained the importance of education to them all at a young age. One day everything changed for me.

My ten-year-old son was having constant headaches. They were so bad he would sleep all day and night. I took him to the doctor and she brushed it off. We moved and I had to find a new doctor for my children, and this one did not take my now almost-twelve-year-old son's headaches lightly. He ordered some tests and I thought we would find out what it was and fix it. That was not the case. The first test did not show anything, but the doctor was persistent and ordered a CAT scan of his brain. I started to think there was nothing wrong with him.

I had enrolled in college and was preparing for my first week of classes when I received the call that every parent dreads. When they call you back the same day or the next day after a test, you know it isn't good. The nurse told me I needed to come in and speak with the neurologist. I knew something was up. As my eyes started to fill with tears, my son ran up to me. I tried to suck up my tears - as if you can do that! But I told him to be quiet as I set an appointment for him the next day. I quickly called his dad to inform him; he seemed not to have a care in the world. I was in full panic mode at that time. My baby had something wrong with his brain.

It turned out my son had a cavernous hemangioma, or cerebral cavernous malformation. That means blood vessels had gathered together and formed some kind of a knot, which is a benign tumor. I lost it! I was in the doctor's office alone because I needed a full understanding of what was going on. I immediately sent an email to my church family, asking for prayers for my baby. I told his father the seriousness of his condition and the fact that the doctor wanted to do an MRI, then surgery if necessary. He said he could not come and to only call him at certain times of a day.

I know what you are thinking. "Well, she has four kids and they are probably not all his." Actually, three of them are his - my oldest three. In any case, I thought he should not be so thoughtless about his child's life.

Fast forward to the day of his surgery. The doctors informed me they would have to perform the actual surgery at their sister location next door because the tumor was so deep they did not have the proper equipment to see it. My sister and I, along with my family in another state, my church family, friends, and Facebook friends prayed hard before his surgery, during, and after. There was only me and my sister along with my three other children at the hospital. I was in full protective mode. I did not want anyone else there, too scared that if they sneezed in the same room as him, it would get worse.

The doctor came out of surgery and explained that the tumor was too deep. They could not remove it without possibly causing some significant damage to his brain. One had busted, but the other one was still intact. The doctor wanted to watch him and have me bring him in on a regular basis and perform MRIs to make sure nothing had changed.

The entire time I was in and out of the hospital with my son, I was still enrolled in school. I told my dad I should just quit, and he told me if it truly mattered to me, I would stay. I could take my hand and play it right and be blessed.

After three years of back and forth with my oldest son, I was able to complete college and earned my Bachelor's degree in Marketing. With all the in and out of hospitals, I could barely keep a job, so walking across the stage was not an option because I just could not afford it. I had three other children to provide for too and little-to-no child support, if any. I leaned on my parents often to help me as well as my little brother, but as luck would have it, I found a job and I was able to go back to work with an employer who understood my circumstances. My son was doing better, and I was working and bringing in my own money, needing my parents' and brother's help a lot less.

And then something happened with my baby boy.

He was always a little different, but I am weird to people, so I thought nothing of it. My son had just started kindergarten and the teacher would send home notes stating he was cursing her out and trying to run from the school, or that he'd taken all his clothes off and thrown things in the classroom. I was very upset with my son, so I would punish him. Nothing seemed to work. He would not interact with his peers and he did not show emotion unless he was upset. His teacher suggested I get him tested and stated in a nice way that he might need to be seen by a therapist. Given the things I had experienced, I made an appointment. The therapist was ready to get my son a check and get us out of his office. I guess he'd never seen a parent like me because I needed to know what was wrong with my son, not get a check from the government. I went for a second opinion. When he was finally seen, I was told my baby boy had schizophrenia and Asperger's Disorder. This doctor stated that schizophrenia in children his age is very rare. He was eight at the time of his diagnosis. My son talked about his "friends" often at that time also.

The constant doctor visits and therapy sessions were hard, but I remembered what my dad said. Having higher education was my dream. I enrolled back into college in the midst of going through this.

Finding the right medication for my son was hard. The school always called me and I often had to pick my son up from school and bring him with me to work. This was something I was told was okay, but the fact that it happened a lot made my superiors have a change of heart. I started missing work and eventually lost that job, but I kept pressing on. I was without work this last time for two years. In that time, I kept my studies going. I took my oldest to his regular MRI visits and went on a medication trail with my youngest, which seemed like an eternity. I kept praying that my oldest would be cleared to play football, and he was. I kept praying that my other son would find a medication that would work and we did.

In the midst of all of the difficulties with my sons, I thought I had found love again. I'd met this guy as a child at church and never given him a second thought, until years later when I finally joined Facebook. It started off innocent - little notes in my inbox. I thought nothing of it until he asked me for my number. After giving it much thought, I decided to go ahead and give him my number. What harm could giving him my digits do? Little did I know...

This man (I'll call him Shorty) was charming, handsome, and not a shy bone in his body. He knew what he wanted and he set out to get it. He started off by texting me - you know, those "Good Morning, Beautiful" texts. Soon the texts turned into calls and we would talk for hours. I started to do what most of us young women do: "catch feelings". I tried to hide those because I did not want to be caught up.

Shorty apparently did a lot of things that I had no idea about. He had been shot, been to jail for fighting, and he had it in his mind that he was a pimp. I thought he had changed, of course, just going off the eight- and ten-hour conversations we would have in a day. He seemed like a good man.

Shorty and I stayed on the phone or computer. I could barely work because my time was so consumed with him, even though he was a 1,000 miles away. Shorty and I finally made it official. Six months after making our relationship official, Shorty came to visit. Since we are both from the same area, he decided to go home and visit for the Christmas holidays since I told him I go home every year for Christmas.

After months of waiting and anticipating, I finally got a chance to see Shorty in person and introduce him to my children. Shorty and I went on our first date, which was riding around town in his mom's car. We talked and laughed, kissed and rubbed on each other like teenagers. Then we finally did the-damn-thang.

In the middle of all that hot and steamy sex, he said he wanted to remain friends, then he nutted all inside me. That made the sex not so good any more. I started to back away. I ignored his calls the next day mainly because I was so hurt and confused. All that time I'd spent with him only to find out I was just a piece of ass. How did I not see this?

I was barely speaking to Shorty - until I took a test and found out I was pregnant. There was no doubt in my mind he was the father. Why did I not make him wear a condom? He was supposed to be my boyfriend, and if you are in a committed relationship, your boyfriend does not wear condoms. What was I going to do?

I informed Shorty that I was pregnant and of course he said I could not say for sure it was his child. That hurt me even more. Although we had only had sex one time, we did not use a contraceptive. I told Shorty I needed a break from him to get my head together. He was not happy about that, but he gave me a day - that was all he gave me. That one day I had to myself, I went to the doctor and found out I was carrying twins. This was a blow to me, and no, I wasn't thinking about my children. I was thinking about Shorty's response to that news. Shorty said twins didn't run in his family, as if that was an automatic, "YOU ARE NOT THE FATHER."

I went into a depression. In that state of mind, I lost one of my babies. After being treated for the miscarriage, you would have thought Shorty would have come up to comfort me, but he did not. I started seeing a person I had not seen in the beginning. About a week after my miscarriage, my first cousin passed away. That hurt like nothing else. My cousin shared my birthday and was like my big brother. Although Shorty did not come up for the miscarriage, he was there for me via phone for my cousin's passing. That meant everything to me - until I lost my other baby. I suffered three losses and the man I loved so deeply never came.

I was so lost in love with the image Shorty presented that I totally overlooked the true man who was staring me right in my face. I had warnings from family members and friends, but I did not listen. Always look for action behind the words. Never be so desperate for love that you allow the trickster in.

I'm still a single mom. I completed my grad degree in Human Resource Management, and I am currently working for the state with young adults. I am finally on my desired career path.

You can achieve anything you set out to do! If you feel discouraged, remember to:

1.   Always pray in everything you do and be optimistic no matter how negative situations you encounter might be.

2.   Meditate or read something Biblical for inspiration and encouragement.

3.   NEVER QUIT! Do not listen to naysayers. Go hard for yourself.

God does truly give the hardest battles to those He knows can handle it. You may not see it, but keep pressing on, keep praying, keep showing love, and your success will come. Go get your blessings!

Edwanna Smoot

Edwanna Smoot is a single mother of four beautiful children from a rural town in Louisiana by the name of Varnado. She has a Master's degree in Human Resources and a Bachelor's in Marketing and Advertising, but most importantly, she is a child of God. It is through God that she found her true propose.

She is here to serve and believes a story untold hinders not just her, but those around her. She has survived mental and physical abuse, loneliness, anger, mother/daughter issues, and not knowing who she truly is. She believes that in order to love on purpose, you must first love yourself - the good, the bad, and the ugly parts of you - and then you will step into your destiny.

www.twitter.com/naturalblckbell
Email: smoot_edwanna@yahoo.com

Battlefield of a Ready Warrior
Charlotte Brazzle

I was born in the small town of Bogalusa, Louisiana, as the sixth child out of fifteen siblings. I was raised in Redmond Heights, which wasn't the roughest area in the projects, but life was still hard. People would move to Redmond Heights one day, and a few weeks later, they'd move out. The new people would complain that the neighborhood was too rough and that the kids were a bad influence. The projects taught us children how to survive in the streets. We played cards, shot dice, and wouldn't hesitate to throw a punch. We knew how to defend ourselves. It was a poverty-stricken area with a bunch of parents trying to make it with their kids.

We were raised in a Pentecostal Church where proper girls wore long dresses down to their ankles. You didn't dare talk to boys in church, the women warned us. They would always tell us, "Jesus is watching," and the idea of God's eyes seeing my every move in church scared me. I became a tomboy because I liked being around boys, but I didn't want to be considered fast.

Life got more difficult as my siblings and I grew older. Redmond Heights became a much-more dangerous place for us as we transitioned into adulthood. In 1975 I lost one of my baby brothers. He was shot in the head by accident and died on his way to hospital because the ambulance broke down. Five months later, my oldest brother got framed and killed by racist white men. They were jealous of how strong and successful my brother was becoming, and set him up for a crime to get caught. While he was in jail, a day after my mother had just visited him, he was killed. Our family struggled to process the fact that we were down to fourteen living children. Our family never recovered from losing those two lights in our lives.

In high school, I didn't care too much about grades. My four surviving older siblings had moved out and I was the oldest child in the house. In 1979 I messed around and got pregnant. I felt God had blessed me with a bundle of joy. Mama didn't agree. She was so angry and put me out of the house because I didn't want go back to school. I confessed to my favorite sibling, my second oldest sister, what happened with the baby and school. She promised to come and get me to stay with her, and I stayed with a friend for a few months while I waited for her.

On October 19, 1979, my sister was killed while on a road trip to Vegas. My mother chose to bury my sister on my birthday, which still bothers me today. I hurt so badly that I took drinking and smoking weed from an occasional, social thing to another level in order to block out reality. Twelve years went by with me barely making it. My job was just enough to pay bills. In 1992, my dad was diagnosed with cancer. I was a daddy's girl and stuck by his side every step of the way. I still remember when he died on March 3rd at about 11:00 at night. A few days later, I was once again back in a cemetery, trying to figure out why God was so mad at my family.

Drinking and smoking wasn't enough to keep me going anymore. I made the mistake of telling this to a girlfriend of mine who decided to "help" me by giving me some stronger stuff. It started with weed laced with cocaine powder. One day she came to my house and I thought we were going to smoke weed again. I was good and tipsy when she held a pipe to my mouth. I cooperated with my own downfall, by sucking in the smoke. Crack cocaine took my mind to another level. After that first taste, I left the laced weed behind and graduated to only smoking crack, until it began to take control of me.

In 1994, another one of my baby brothers got shot. He'd been in line outside of a club and got caught in the crossfire between rival gang members. Less than a year later, another baby brother got killed in Houston, Texas, in a drug deal gone bad. We later found out that a contract had been put on him. I adopted an "I don't give-a-damn" mind frame. I felt death would come for me too, so what ever happened to me just happened. By this time, I'd lost four brothers, my father, and my favorite sister. I became so ANGRY with God, I called him everything but God. I dared anyone I knew to try to comfort me with talks about heaven or God's plan. I'd scream at them and insist He didn't exist.

I'd been on crack for a little over a year. By that time, I felt so dead inside and had very few morals. My idea of hustling was no longer working hard. Instead, I'd pick men's pockets. When men tried to get with me, I would laugh and flirt, just so I could drink them under the table. I snuck a few eye drops into whatever my victim was drinking, and he'd always end up passed out in a quiet spot. I'd then clean his wallet out and I didn't have to lay with any of them. This game was going good for a long time - until someone figured out what I was doing. I had to stop stealing from the guys at bars. Instead, I met them at bars and let them drink a lot more than me. Later, I had my infatuated-marks meet me at a motel. While I was pouring them gin and juice, I poured myself water and juice. We'd then take off our clothes and have sex. If I was lucky, the men were so drunk, I never had to do much more than mess around before they passed out. Either way, the men didn't know I had someone waiting in the room to get the money from their pants while we had our transaction.

I really started to hate myself and became determined not to use my body. I tried going straight and began to clean up at the local bar and wash cars to make money, but it was never enough to support my habit. I started to sell on the side and connected with a new man, Joe. We dated about a year before he asked me to marry him. Even though I hadn't been around him that long, I was delighted with the idea of being married. I said yes. A few months into the marriage, Joe began to beat me, first with his fists, then he graduated to beating me over the head with a pistol while choking me. I didn't try to fight back because he'd hurt me more. I eventually got to the point where I wanted him to kill me.

Joe was always in a rage. By that time, he was selling and smoking too. The beatings got worse because he wanted me to go back to prostitution and I wouldn't go sleep with the men. Eventually, I gave in, so while the victim and I were in the motel room, Joe would kick in the door and rob the other man. Joe called me a dirty whore because I did what he'd forced me to do. He would beat me in the street, strip me naked, and try to make me perform oral sex on him in the street.

I only got away from Joe after I went to friend's house and took her prescribed sleeping pills. I tried to take every one and passed out. I woke up in the hospital, and after they pumped my stomach, they sent me to jail. I'd had drugs on me and had tested positive for crack cocaine when I'd been in the hospital. I was in jail for three months. My mother actually came to bail me out, but I told her no. I wanted to stay, get rest, and be away from my husband. I was also working with the State on getting Joe prosecuted. A few months later, police arrested him for possession and abuse. Joe went to trial and I testified against him. He was easily convicted. When I got out of jail, I was finally free from him.

The year of 1999 was the worst. I found out my child was really ill, and when I took him to the doctor to find out what was going on with him, they told me he had Hepatitis C. There was so much medication he had to take daily, and he was in and out of hospital for months. However hard he fought the good fight, my child did not survive his sickness long. On July 27, 1999, my son passed away. After the funeral, I was a zombie. So many people had died and now it was time to clock out.

I bought a pistol, put it to my head fully-loaded, and pulled the trigger, but not one bullet came out of its chamber. I threw down the defective weapon and left to buy drugs. My plan was to consume so much crack that my heart would flood then stop beating. I tried snorting and smoking, but nothing happened. I barely even got high. I was so confused. Why couldn't I commit suicide properly?

Eventually, I realized it wasn't my time to die. God wanted me to live. I checked into a rehab facility. I stayed there for six months, then went to New Orleans, then Baton Rouge. One Sunday I called my mom to tell her how good I was doing. I had just gotten a job at Summit Hospital. Then she dropped a bomb on me. She told me she had cancer, so of course I left to take care of her. I did everything possible to make her comfortable for the little time she had. On December 17, 2000, my mother passed and I lost it. I got right back on that roller coaster ride with crack. I was so addicted that I sold everything and stole people's stuff. It got so bad, I had nowhere to stay or take a bath.

One Sunday, I was just walking. I didn't know where I was going. That was the day I met Duke. He invited me to stay at his place with no strings attached. I didn't care too much about anything at the time, so I took him up on his offer. He didn't see me as a worthless crackhead, and when I got cleaned up, he wanted to have a relationship with me. We got along so well that I stayed with him for two years, but guess who eventually popped up at our doorstep? Joe, the nightmare, stood there, ready to ruin my life again. Joe had gotten out of jail, found out where Duke and I lived, and came to the house wanting to meet Duke.

I wasn't afraid of Joe anymore. God had given me a man who loved and respected me, so I was not going to let Joe try to hurt our relationship. I sucker-punched Joe and I ran to get my gun. I didn't shoot him, but I did pistol-whip Joe until he was knocked out. I then called the police to come get him. When the police came, I gave one officer my gun. I later told Duke, that if Joe came near me again, I'd have to kill him, so Duke and I decided to start life in a new place. We left Bogalusa with the clothes on our backs and fifteen dollars in our pockets.

I thank God for Duke, but in 2006, I left him in Florida and moved to Denver for a while, to be by myself where I rededicated my life to God. I now know I needed that period alone with God, so I could realize that HE has called those I love to heaven because they are His to take. I, however, survived so much pain so I'd have a story to tell. People will be blessed by my story.

I have been clean and sober for ten years, filled with the Holy Ghost, and walking in purpose and with a plan that God has for my life, to be an example to others. My suffering was necessary. I had to go through those experiences because all things work for my good. My son left this world at the age of twenty, but I thank God for the time I had with him. He left me a grandson, and he is my blessing. I know I'm like a modern day Job. I was tested by God so I could save a many people who are suffering and need guidance.

Charlotte Smith-Brazzle

Charlotte Smith-Brazzle was born in the small town of Bogalusa, Louisiana, as the sixth child out of fifteen siblings. She attended Pasadena Adult Center, where she got her high school diploma in 2009, then went on to Everest Institute of Houston, TX. She graduated in 2010 with certification as a medical assistant. In 2012, she decided to finish her education by attending San Jacinto College.

Charlotte is an evangelist, author, Minister of Music, and an entrepreneur.

You can contact Charlotte at:

dukelady4life60@gmail.com

A Warrior Was Already Within Me
Paulina Armstrong

My childhood, for the most part, was filled with lots of fun, happiness, and love, but it also consisted of pain, hurt, and tears. Growing up in a household with three wonderful sisters and both parents was a dream to me. Some people around me weren't raised in a two-parent home, so I considered us fortunate - not to say that others weren't fortunate as well, but to me, that meant everything. I enjoyed being raised in the Coney Island section of Brooklyn, New York. My life was pretty good from a child's perspective, but somewhere in my early teens, what was perceived as being pretty good turned to bad. Our happy household was turned upside down from all types of abuse.

I didn't understand it back then, but as I got older, I recognized the irrational behavior as being a generational curse that plagued several family members as well. My childhood has made me sensitive to others who have gone through similar situations or witnessed some type of abuse. Abuse doesn't just affect the intended victim, but anyone else who is a witness. It shakes you to the core of your being. The pain that I experienced during my childhood was packed up with me as I matured into a young woman and carried around in an invisible backpack throughout my adult life.

My childhood pain didn't help me in my relationships with the opposite sex because I was so defensive, and I believed if I showed my true self, I would be hurt because of it. One thing was important to me during my teen years: I would focus solely on making sure that academically I was doing the best I could do. I've loved to read books ever since I was a little girl, so I used books as a temporary escape from real life during my early teens. During junior high school and high school, cigarettes and beer were first introduced into my life. Because of what I was experiencing at home, it was nothing to me to submit to peer pressure, to feel as if I was finally someone who didn't have any issues; the cigarettes and alcohol temporarily took the place of the pain. One of the happiest moments of my teen years was graduating from high school and landing a job at Dime Savings Bank as a teller after making bad choices academically.

As a mature eighteen-year-old, I was excited to have completed this accomplishment and to be a member of the workforce. During that time, I met a young man who I was interested in getting to know as a friend. My father was a strict disciplinarian who did not allow his daughters to socialize with the opposite sex, which I never understood, so I had to sneak to visit my new male friend. We became friends - or at least, that's what I believed. One day, he began to fondle me, which was completely new to me since I was a virgin. All I kept hearing in my head was my mother's voice telling me to keep my legs closed, so I told him to stop, but I guess to him, stop meant go, and he forcefully took my virginity from me. Now back then, I didn't know anything about the word "rape" so I didn't associate what happened to me as rape. I took the whole incident and suppressed it as if it never happened. I never told anyone about what happened to me, until a friend recently asked me if something forceful happened to me when I was younger because of how I had reacted to something that was said to me. When I thought about it, it brought tears to my eyes. I guess I'm still being affected by something I thought was buried, but now has resurfaced through my words and actions.

As much as I didn't want to publicly share my testimony, it isn't about me, but what God has called me to do, which is to put others first. Through my trials, through my pain, through my insecurities, through my tears, it is all to help someone else to get through their trials and tribulations, just as I have. My pain will become my strength through my testimony. I want to share this quote: "When we speak, we are afraid our words will not be heard or welcomed. But when we are silent, we are still afraid. So it is better to speak." - *Audra Lorde*

Life isn't all about the good times, but also the bad times. The difference on how you deal with both is in your perspective. You can either choose to lie down in defeat, or you can choose to fight for the life you know you deserve. Has my life been filled with only happiness? Not at all. But through the grace of God, I made it through every single trial and tribulation. I've been in situations where I felt as if I was the only one going through afflictions. God has truly kept me and protected me even when I didn't know I was being kept. There are so many times the enemy tried to kill me - literally - but God said "no". I'm so grateful because He is my protector and refuge. I should have been dead five times, but God spared my life for such a time as this. I'm here to encourage others and show the love of Christ.

Trials and struggles aren't all bad for us. They can also be good for us. Trials and struggles teach us how to have total dependence on God, how to have perseverance, and how to endure. Trials aren't just for us as individuals, but for others as well. What you go through as a person can help someone else who may be going through something as well and who may need encouragement and hope to know it will be alright. Trials and struggles also help you to build character, such as discipline, humility, and hope.

There was a season in my life where I didn't feel pretty enough. I was so insecure inside, but the people around me could never tell because I refused to show it. There were many times I just cried myself to sleep because I didn't understand what God was doing during that sad season of my life. As I look back now and ponder it, God was showing me how to be humble and to be patient, which was something I really struggled with for a long time. When I finally told God I trust Him and truly believed the words I said to Him, God really started to work on and in me. My spiritual journey has cost me friendships because of my obedience to the Word of God and the fact that I'm not ashamed of the gospel. If I had the chance to go back to the life I lived previously…would I? Absolutely not! I just want to tell someone out there who is reading this right now to be encouraged in the Lord. He will never leave you nor forsake you.

You are here for a reason, and although you may or may not know what the reason is, just know your life has purpose and meaning. The life you desire is tangible. If you can believe it, then you can have it. You are beautiful. You are powerful inside and out. You are unique. You are special and loved by God. Don't waste your potential, because God has placed in all of us gifts and talents. Become the woman God intended you to be. There is greatness in you and the world needs to see it. Never settle or apologize for having standards. Don't ever quit and give up. Keep the faith and don't lose hope. Your past is behind you and so is your past shame, regret, and guilt. Don't let your failures get you down. Get back up ready for round two. You're stronger than you think you are.

Don't let people or circumstances define who are you are. You are who God has called you to be and He doesn't change His mind about your purpose. I know you may not see it or even believe it, but God has allowed certain things to happen to bring you to where you are today. Whatever you go through in life will never be wasted because God will use the things in your life to bless others. Believe in your dreams and watch God make the impossible possible, as long as you trust and believe Him. You were created to be victorious in all you do. You have what it takes to make it! You can do all things through Christ who strengthens you (Philippians 4:13).

Don't allow anyone to downplay what is in you because you are a warrior who makes it rock. We are here to be light in the darkness, to uplift others in their struggles. We are here to build each other up by speaking encouraging words to one another and building up hope so no one is left out or left behind. We are our sisters' keepers (1 Thessalonians 5:11).

Love Reigns Supreme

Love comes in many forms: trust, protection, patience, kindness, humility, forgiveness, unselfishness, and holiness. Love breaks down rejection, sadness, and low self-esteem. Love breaks the chains that hold people in captivity, whether it is physically, mentally, emotionally, or spiritually. Love sustains us, feeds us, and rejuvenates us by bringing joy into our lives. Love is respect, friendship, understanding, communication, and companionship. Love and Respect go hand in hand, and having both can improve your life:

1.　Women should love and respect themselves and others because integrity is everything.

2.　Women should love and respect themselves and others because we are worthy of it.

3.　How you treat others says a lot about you, and you can show others how to treat you, themselves, and others. There are blessings for you when you love and respect others.

4. Although some people may not deserve it because of their behavior towards you or others, we still need to show love and respect to them because it shows a reflection of your character.

I pray that this quote blesses you:

"Everyone has inside them a piece of good news. The good news is you don't know how great you can be! How much you can love! What you can accomplish! And what your potential is."

~ Anne Frank

Paulina Armstrong

Paulina Armstrong is a native New Yorker and resides in Brooklyn, New York. She has two wonderful sons named Demetris (Michi) and Bijan. She is the oldest daughter of four children. She graduated from John Dewey High School. During her employment with the USPS, she is committed to always going above and beyond for her customers. She shows love and kindness to all those that she comes in contact with. Her customers have no problem sharing their own personal trials and tribulations with her because they know they will receive an encouraging word and prayer.

Paulina is a social expert and an inspirational advocate who loves to inspire people. Paulina spends her time serving others through various ministries at church. She is committed to volunteering at a nursing home once a month with other church members. Paulina has also volunteered and served on the Parent Association Board. Paulina is determined to make a huge difference by impacting others through the church by readily being available to serve in whatever capacity needed.

A Beast Spreads Darkness; A Warrior Spreads Light!
Nichole Peters

Living Nightmares

In my mind, in my body, and even in my spirit, I am covered in complete darkness. I float in a womb of blackness, much like a fetus, not quite ready to be born. However, the darkness isn't comforting or safe. I feel trapped, alone, and scared.

OMG, I think. *It's so dark in here. Where am I?*

I'm spiritually naked and afraid, shaking; hot urine is running down my legs, and I can't see. I am blinded in fear, my mind is wiped, almost gone, and I fear I am losing the battle with the darkness.

I am soooo weak. I fight to think and to breathe. My lungs struggle to force air, in and out, in and out. The enemy is like a smothering blanket of soul-sucking blackness. It blinds and chokes me. He pulls and pushes me toward death. I can feel the scorching embers of hellish heat ready to burn me alive.

Up until a decade ago, I would wake up from living, literal nightmares and start coughing as if I was choking on water, or maybe ashes. I felt the night terrors were real, and after experiencing the Brooms-fire in dreams, I would wake up actually smelling like dirty sweat and smoke. All over my body my muscles ached from fighting in my sleep.

What the hell?

He, the nameless demon, had warned me that I was nothing but a stupid, filthy, ugly, and worthless piece of trash. He haunted me in the dead of night and constantly used the dreamscape to trap me away from restful dreams. My spirit self was hidden, floating near the bottom of an immense pit of his suffocating darkness, in a smothering pit of living hell. He had warned me if I didn't follow his every command, thought or wish, he would make me experience real hell forever. I would whimper and try to protect myself from the beast who was kicking my ass!

I was so young and so hopelessly lost. During my waking hours, I shuffled through my days and held onto life by a very thin thread. My existence was filled with so much agony and anger that I'd often overly protect myself. My lack of power and self-control caused me to feel unhappy, unloved, broken, and wounded. Most of all, I was trapped in bondage. I felt like heavy chains weighed me down and wrapped around my neck like a noose. I tried to fight the depression, turmoil, and demonic presence that dwelled inside, and I ended up losing the battle every single time. There were plenty of days I tried to bind the evil that tried to drive me to death or insanity, but again and again, satan proved to me he was a BOSS.

I prayed to the good Lord.

"Father God, I am on my knees, begging you to break me lose from this sick, evil-minded spirit that wants to control my life, keep me in bondage, and send me to his hell. How can I break lose? How do I fight this evil giant?"

I was suffering and I knew the feeling of sick hopelessness didn't originate from any person; the feeling came from the evil principalities that tried to inject satan's deadly darkness like an infection. The spiritual virus attempted to spread all over me. After a few years of being infected, I became even weaker and extremely vulnerable. The evil infection of darkness had penetrated my cells, filled me with rage and grief. I felt abused and let-down as the demon tried to turn me into his creature. After experiencing the dark side of spiritual warfare, I became rebellious like never before, an animalistic version of Nikki in beast mode.

The Mask Is OFF; Welcome to My Inner Beast

In beast mode, I was Nikki-Lee, and boy, boy, boy… I was fierce and ready to attack everything I thought was against me. I was a savage who retaliated against anything or anyone trying to hurt me. I feared nothing in the physical or spiritual realm, and satan knew I was destined to be spiritually-strong. Instead of using that strength for Father God, as a general in the front line of heaven, the enemy took over and forced me to be on his side. His darkness had finally blinded me, and I became that-chick so many people were afraid to mess with. I wasn't so far gone that I started trouble, but if trouble came to me? I would not back down!

I was living that "'bout that life" way. Everything I did was in beast mode. After all those nightmares, let-downs, and after losing almost all the people I loved, I became my own worst nightmare.

On the streets I picked up bad habits. Let me give you a few examples. I became a dope man's first-hand chick. I was a woman trapped by darkness, so being in a relationship with a notorious drug dealer made us a dishonorable team, like Bonnie and Clyde. Did we kill anyone? NO... Let me make that clear now. But we were down for each other and I stood by him every single day. I loved him. I thought living hardcore was the best way, instead of living for God. The inner demon was satisfied, so I didn't suffer inner turmoil or pain when I lived the dark lifestyle. In darkness I became a part of the drug game myself by being his right-hand chick.

Listen... When you come from out the projects, having maybe $5.00 a day, and graduate to a lifestyle where your man is giving you thousands of dollars a day, it's easy to get trapped. I also was an unsurpassed gambler who won and lost big money in casinos. I gambled so much, I practically lived there, so my personal casino host would put me up in five-star suites and give me free vouchers to eat and drink. The way I smoked marijuana you would think I grew trees in my backyard, but I didn't. I was totally stressing, and smoking was a way for me to ease the pain, have happy thoughts, elevate my appetite, and get me some good sleep. I became a blinded flunky in love. Often times I would ride with him to make sure no other "hot-girl" was by his side. We'd follow behind the traffickers to deliver supplies all over the south for many of the big dealers, including some who were dirty police officers!

I had obviously lost my-freaking-mind. The enemy had me in his power, which made me feel powerless to escape. There were temptations. I thrived on making money and money became mammon. (Mammon is any wealth that comes from an evil influence or anything you idolize and put before GOD.) Money was nothing to me. My man made it and we spent it. I felt safe because I was protected by his posse, in addition to being protected by a few dirty cops.

My man's job was so dirty, I even had to carry my Glock daily, because when you in those streets, you have to be prepared for the worse. There's a saying that goes, "You live by the streets, you die by the streets." I wasn't ready to lie down and die, so I was ready for whatever came my way.

When I lived in the darkness, I didn't suffer from the demonic nightmares that had haunted me for over a decade, nor was I suicidal, depressed, or even distressed. I no longer felt worthless or stupid. People respected me because I was street-famous, and I felt so much love from those living the dark life with me. My inner beast dwelled in the wilderness of the streets. The darkness was a spirit that controlled my actions, and I was unaware that my actions were so out of control and shameful. I was partly responsible for supplying two of the transformational co-authors in this book, because I chose to stay with him out of love and loyalty. I didn't open up my mouth to tell him, "No! Don't supply them."

Eventually, I woke up from my false sense of safety and peace, and realized I had to stop. Being in beast mode was extremely dangerous and I didn't want to end up in jail or dead. I decided I needed to hear God's voice. I needed guidance and started praying, but when I tried, I felt such horrible pain. It felt like somebody was ripping my guts out. My heart pumped slowly, and I could barely breathe. Attempting to pray stressed my nerves so badly I'd vomit and suffer with migraine headaches. I was being tortured, just like the spiritual version of myself in the dreamscape.

Breaking Free

As my babies grew older, I attempted to get myself together and get an honest job. After going to court, the truth was revealed, and I was pardoned from all felony drug charges. However, I knew I couldn't afford to stay around that kind of environment. I became determined to end my long-term relationship and disassociate myself from a few people. I had to ignore the unsettling feelings of wrenching pain and the demonic voice mocking my efforts to do better.

I avoided the people who wanted me to stay trapped, but every single time I got a position that was worth a grain of salt, one particular dirty cop named

Detective Harold, who knew and was highly upset with me, interfered. He wanted me to keep my hands dirty; so, to make my life difficult, he took a copy of the newspaper article of when I was arrested to my legitimate jobs and told them they should never let me work there. He grinned as he gave them all the reasons why they should fire me. That dirty cop cost me two major job opportunities! I'd been groomed for a loan officer position at a bank through Keenan Staffing the first time he sought to ruin me. The second time was at a clothing store where I was being considered for an assistant manager position. I was cut loose from both jobs once they heard from him. This sent me back in a rage and in beast mode again! I felt like no matter what I did, I was set up for failure. I was a loser, just like the evil one had said. I tried not to despair as the demon sent visions of his imps and snakes to try to destroy my mind and my true life's purpose.

The cop was highly upset that I beat every charge in the court. He vowed vengeance against me because he'd bullied me to give up information I had on the "big dog". I had lied to him instead of telling him what I knew. I didn't believe in being a snitch or an informant. I just wanted out!

Even after I had given up the lifestyle on the streets and had rededicated my life to GOD, the dirty cop wouldn't let me breathe. He wanted me back, dwelling in the darkness. I refused to work around anything illegal again, even though he had cost me my good jobs, but this cop wouldn't stop! Detective Harold threatened me in every way he could to get me to confess everything I might know, all while his hypocritical behind supplied confiscated drugs to dealers and slept with the same drug-users and girls my man supplied in the same city. This cop wasn't new to the game and moved way more product than my man's posse ever did. He just never met the top supplier because the big dog didn't trust cops. And it was good the big man didn't trust this particular cop. Detective Harold wasn't loyal; he was so dirty that he often set people up to get caught if he didn't get his way or get his cut. I refused to give-in to his blackmail, so he had it out for me, but Madear didn't raise no fool either!

I was one of the few who finally started using common sense and wisdom. I knew there was no way he could get me in trouble if I stayed away from certain people and places. I was living clean, so I took a stand and said

ENOUGH! He hated my confidence and my defiance, and tortured me any way he could. He, or one of his bad ol' officers, often stopped my car to give me unnecessary tickets, that even now I have never paid. The cops taunted me, trying to make me say or do something, like threaten them back, so Detective Harold could justify his actions in arresting me. He wouldn't back down, so I stood my ground and used my old connections to fight back against him. I became involved in a federal investigation that helped take Detective Harold down, by blowing the whistle on one of the biggest drug deals down south. I had asked him over and over again to leave me ALONE! But pleading with the devil doesn't work. The demonic thrives on weakness, so I had to fight back to gain my freedom from harassment and from a future on the streets this dirty cop wanted me to have.

I had a plan for satan now. I was determined to do more than ignore the pain. I decided to fight for the light, on God's side of the battlefield, and from that point on, I became an unstoppable force!

The hardest part was breaking away from the people and posse I considered like family. Even though they lived and made money in a way that wasn't right, they were God's children too, and I had felt loved. I'd only been active in the streets a few years, but I knew it would be a struggle to break all ties completely, especially after selecting the wrong relationships in my life. I made sure my children were safe by letting them stay with my mother (aka Ma'Dear) as I worked to change my life.

I had no problem finding and keeping, a normal job with the dirty cops out of the picture. My work ethic and drive has been impeccable since I was 9 years old. As a child, I'd convinced my big sister Vanessa to sign up for Avon because I was too young. I then took the Avon books and samples around to every project door and sold Skin-So-Soft products in record numbers. At the age of 14, I got my first official paycheck working with a government low-income program called JTPA. At age 17, my friends Melinda, Will, and I were working at Covington Burger King, 30 minutes from Bogalusa, until I went off to college. I also held a cashier job working for Wally World for a many of years.

During my college years, I held other jobs. One was on campus under the federal school program and my second job was at Popeye's. I juggled these two jobs and struggled to take my classes until I met my student tutor one semester. I thought I'd met the man of my dreams, a perfectly-respectable man who could teach me to be successful. Instead, he introduced to me to a world on the streets I never knew existed.... But at the end of the day I took full responsibility for my life without blaming anyone because I could've said NO!

Don't Judge Me

I bet there are some people who know a little about me, who are now reading this chapter and are dropping their jaws. Well... breathe in and out, slowly close your mouth, and place your hand over heart. It was time I'll let you all know why I fight and go hard daily to help so many young women who are TRAPPED, hanging in the traps, and think the only love out there exists in the streets. I MUST SPEAK LIFE daily to every Woman who is blinded by darkness. The mask has finally come off.

WHEW.... I am not afraid or ashamed to tell you about the mistakes I've made, the burdens I've bore, and the struggles I went through. My story is my GLORY for GOD and His people who need help!!! I will never let anyone make me feel inferior, embarrassed, or crazy for telling about my past life. Once the voice of Father God told me to go forth, I listened, and Jesus forgave me of my sins. Proverbs 3:5 says, "Trust in the LORD with all your heart and lean not on your own understanding." I know that Father God has called me to spread the light and reach many other WARRIORS! My Spiritual leaders told me I needed to let my light shine and reach the wounded, and my purpose-driven leader said to "Come Out of Hiding and Shine." I knew the best way to release all the lingering doubts and fears was to turn my story of darkness into a journey towards glorious light.

I was broken inside and required truth to open my eyes and now spread the gift of true sight to other lives. So to the holier-than-thou types who may question my past... How can I help anyone with my testimony without telling the truth? The hell with that! I must SPEAK LIFE, and remove the MASK! I am now FREE. I am now at PEACE and have BROKEN THROUGH every trial satan has thrown at me so far.

Beyond Expectations

If anyone is disappointed by my past, I am sorry. I've given my past to Father God. I have made mistakes that have affected my loved ones, so I apologize, especially to my children and my Ma'Dear. Just know everything happens for a reason and some are bad choices turned into blessings. We may choose the wrong path, but if we don't break, God can turn our struggles into strengths. Every last one of us on this earth steps out of order, and I sincerely believe I have taken steps in these shoes for a reason. Father God tells us our steps are all ordered.

Right now, to this day, I do outreach and check on some of my old posse, homies, and friends who I know will make it off the streets one day soon. I do the same as Jesus would do... REACH BACK! I truly believe I have experienced life in so many ways so I can help many types of people in this world.

Why I was picked to bear the burden of such darkness was a puzzle for me, until I realized satan knew I had the ability, to one day, break every chain he tried to choke me with. He knew Nikki Woman was going to rise up and help Jesus save the world! He hoped I would fall down and never discover my true, God-given strength, but, thank the Lord, I eventually GOT UP!!!

He knew I would eventually WARRIOR UP... and win.

Father GOD did it!

Nichole Peters

People are allowed to have their own opinions, and how they may feel about me after I spoke my truth is something I said I would respect. However, don't attempt to judge me. Don't throw stones. Sin is sin. We all sin or have sinned in our own unique way. I've bared my soul because people are in need of powerful testimonies on ways to drive out darkness, on how face your demons, and battle sin. Stories based off truth are necessary to help others, especially women, who may also be trapped in that gangsta lifestyle. I knew I had to Warrior Up and let victims, haters, and stone-throwing naysayers know they can all change and become great too! Anything is possible for those who believe in our Father God. Your transformation can take place no matter what you've been through…

You can open up your light and spread it all over the world. This is only the beginning!!!

THE WARRIOR HONOREE
FOR GIVING BACK

Dr. Shanta Barton-Stubbs

At the age of twenty-one, I was a sophomore in college in a class full of policemen, studying criminal justice and doing everything possible to become a SWAT team member. I sat there in this class for years and learned the ins and outs of the field. I even witnessed an autopsy being done on a cadaver. Although I was doing well in school and I thought it was what I wanted to do, it was totally different from what I expected. It was beginning to bother me. I didn't jump up every morning going to school, I wasn't excited about the stuff I was learning, and most importantly, I didn't feel the field was really for me.

I grew up seeing my parents give all they had for others, and at times, they were not appreciated for their hard work and sacrifice. I also experienced my parents bringing so many other youths into our home throughout my years of growing up. Sometimes our own lives were interrupted by the good hearts of my parents. I did not want to follow in their exact same footsteps.

One Sunday morning as I sat in church, which had become my every Sunday ritual, the announcement came - the announcement which I thought tore my insides out. We were moving our beautiful congregation to a location in the Parramore Community. *Parramore?* I thought. *Why are we going there?* Although I was familiar with the area, I knew very well that Parramore was not the location where we belonged. When I heard my parents speak about the great work Parramore needed to experience, I began to question them and others as to why God would send us to a desolate place, not recognizing what was about to take place. I kicked and screamed; I questioned God and my parents to be sure this was what we were supposed to do.

I went down to this Parramore place to help my father begin the process of cleaning out the ugliest building I had ever seen. Our chores were set up for us, as there was much cleaning, painting, scraping, and transforming needed. Not only was outside in the community dirty, stinky, and forgotten about, but most people despised the area.

Finally, as we were talking outside, we saw some youths across the street playing in a grocery cart. There was no grocery store in sight, yet, a few of the youths were running in and out of the street, pushing a grocery cart and watching the other youths bump into things, or even fall out of the basket. I began to think it was such a dangerous game, and before I knew it, without even thinking, I began to yell out across the street, "Hey, you, stop doing that! Someone's going to get hurt." The moment it came from my mouth, I remember thinking, *Mind your business, Shanta; this has nothing to do with you.*

Two out of five of the boys stopped, turned to look at me, and began to curse me out and tell me exactly what my mind had told me to do: mind my own business. I was a little surprised that youths this age would talk to adults like that. I walked over as bold as I knew how and said, "Who are you talking to?" When I began to talk to the youths, I recognized they were normal youths doing things youths do to have fun in the neighborhood. I don't even remember the exact words, but I do remember inviting them into my dad's church, into this one room which consisted of the ugliest walls, the smell of mold, and the look of a condemned building. I brought them inside and the only thing available was one game of Monopoly. We played that one game of Monopoly and that's when I began to see the youths come alive. After that game and a few snacks later, I sent the kids home and I ended my day.

A couple of days passed by and my dad called to tell me those youths with whom I had played the game had come back asking for me and asking when I was coming back. I went across the street to what is known as the corner store, and we once again began to fill the day with laughs, jokes, and this game of Monopoly. I'm not sure what happened that day and I'm not sure what that day meant for my youths, but I can tell you something sparked in me. Without even thinking, every day after school, I found myself running down to this mold-infested building in this poverty-stricken neighborhood. I wanted to see the kids and I wanted to expose them to more and more games. Now this was what was considered their summer vacation and I wanted to be sure to give them a lot more fun than what we were doing.

I had $1500 saved in my bank account, I began to use some of it to buy board games from Walmart and video games from pawn shops, along with a used computer. I began to transform that one mold-infested room into something you would call a kids' area. I serviced twelve youths the first few weeks (the word had quickly begun to travel), and now twelve years later, we currently serve over ninety youths in the Parramore community and give them the opportunity to dream. Under my leadership and with the assistance of others, we currently have twenty-one high school graduates and ten students in college. If you had told me years ago my destiny was going to lead me here, I would not have believed you. Just as I have been a blessing to many of our youths, they have also helped shape me into the woman I am today. I went back to school for a Master's degree in Mental Health Counseling to be sure I was assisting our youth in the best way possible. Also, leading by example, I continued on to obtain my doctorate to show the youth, if I could do it, they could do it as well. This amazing story came from that one little place I never knew would become so great or phenomenal, and I even sometimes don't believe the story has come into fruition.

Is this a hard task? Why yes, it is, but our youths are our future and someone has to be willing to take the time out for them and steer them in the right direction. At times, I find it hard trying to balance church, New Image Youth Center, my career, and family, but with God, I know all things are possible. I encourage others to look for opportunities to give back. I am not sure if you are aware of this or not, but we were all put on this earth to serve. Why not serve our youths?

People always ask me why I do this, and how am I successful? I reply, "How are you a parent and yet still manage to come home every day knowing the next day you have to do it again?"

You see, I know I was ordained for this. I didn't know it in the beginning, but the moment God had the kids come into my life, I knew my purpose. It felt right. Late nights, early mornings, 9-1-1 phone calls coming in at all times of the night, those are nothing new to me. No matter what, I still feel humbled that God chose me to be a leader and mentor for His children.

New Image is that one safe place the kids flock to in the hood. I can remember one morning coming to the center at around 7 a.m. and seeing one of my girl students in the backyard with two chairs, stretched out asleep. I woke her up and asked her why was she there. She replied, when her mother went to work, she left to keep her mother's boyfriend from trying to touch her. Another time I came to the center at 1:00 a.m., only to find brothers sleeping in the backyard after being kicked out of a hotel and having nowhere to go. New Image has become that safe place for our youths. I often tell the youths that New Image Youth Center is the good in the hood, so no matter how much bad happens, there is still good in our hood and they should be proud of it.

New Image is a program that provides our youths the chance to participate in activities which they normally could not afford, such as dance, theater, karate, yoga, field trips, and much more. We prepare them for the world and help them recognize their options, whether it is college, tech school, business, or the armed forces.

When I recognized Nichole Peters had chosen me to be the Warrior Woman of the Year, I cried, knowing that God's Word does prevail. God stated that when things are done in secret, He would reward us openly. God has always taken care of me, and I feel so blessed. My prayer now is that He take care of our youths. I can't stand to see people talk about our children and complain about how bad this generation is, yet they do nothing in order to see these youths change.

It has not been easy, but yes, it is all worth it.

I can tell you I have had a lot of breakdown moments, moments of not knowing how we would pay the bills and stand, but God has always made a way. In 2015, one of our students graduated from Morehouse College with the help of his NIYC family. He is currently in the PhD. program at Auburn University. Another student is starting his senior year at Claflin University and graduating with honors. One of our female students is currently the reigning Ms. Teen Florida Excellence Queen.

And to think it all started from a mold-infested building and one confused college student with a mind to highlight the good in the middle of the hood.

Shanta Barton-Stubbs

Dr. Shanta Barton-Stubbs is the founder and director of New Image Youth Center in Orlando, Florida. At the age of twenty-one, Shanta Stubbs founded the New Image Youth Center with only $1,500 and eight children. Shanta now helps mentor over sixty-five children a day in the Parramore Community. Shanta received her undergraduate degree in Criminal Justice, a Master's degree in Mental Health, and in 2015, Shanta received her Doctorate in Bible College, with an emphasis on Leadership Studies.

Shanta has been the recipient of many awards including: the Bank of America Local Hero Award in 2007; the 2008 Magic Maker Award; the 2011 L'Oréal Women of Worth top 10 nominee; and the National Title Miss Corporate America in 2009. Shanta Barton-Stubs is the first African American woman to win this title.

New Image Youth Center has two facilities in the Parramore community along with the addition of a community garden that allows her and her kids to grow organic food for the homeless. Shanta's goal is to be a role model for at-risk youths and women to show they can defy the odds under any circumstances. Shanta is a licensed therapist, a certified Success Life Coach, a motivational speaker, and the founder of Under Construction Empowerment Services, counseling and consulting services, that guides individuals to reaching their goals and to success.

Connect with Shanta at:

www.facebook.com/sbartonstubbs
www.facebook.com/newimageyouthcenter/?pnref=lhc
http://www.newimageyouth.org

Afterword
Claudia Alexander

A warrior has scars. Scars are evidence you fought hard and survived. Scars prove you are a fighter and verify you have not been beaten to the point of no return. But getting them hurts.

I have so many scars, both physical and psychological. My skin scars easily because of a condition called hyperpigmentation. If I get a small cut, a scrape, or mess with a pimple too much, the scar heals in a much-darker tone than my skin. It takes forever for these blemishes to fade and it makes me so self-conscious, so the idea is to keep myself from getting hurt, because scars are ugly.

But what about the psychological scars?

I have many, but so do a lot of other people. After reading all the chapters in this book, I realize that so many beautiful women have experienced so much pain in their lives, yet their spirits have not been broken. That's a beautiful thing. However, dealing with pain means you've been wounded, burned, cut, stabbed, or lynched. You've been left broken, hollow, crying out… and I think, "Why must we bleed to grow stronger?"

You get scars from dealing with the aftermath of a painful relationship. You get scars from rape and molestation and abuse. You get scars from losing loved ones - brothers, sisters, parents, and children who should have buried you. You get scars from making mistakes and trusting the wrong people. You get scars from lying to yourself and hiding the light God put inside you.

Personal Accountability Is Everything

I realized a little over twelve years ago that I couldn't stay quiet about the things that bother me. I used to be a shadow as a child and teen. I accepted my parents' abuse because I got the arguing and protests beaten out of me. I learned it didn't matter that I wasn't involved in my siblings' hijinks. When the lamp is broken and you're the eldest? Your ass is grass. If I got a bad grade? I'm smart, so I must be neglecting my work. If I was late? I'd wasted everyone's time. I got beaten for it all… every mistake I made and some I never did. So I expect to be blamed for everything stupid I've done. I call myself stupid too, and isn't that just dumb?

I ruin most of my relationships because I am scared to trust men. I purposely sabotage everything by being an utter idiot when I should have a man so deeply devoted and in love with me. I sometimes feel hopeless, like my heart is broken into a thousand tiny pieces. *Yeah,* I think. *Maybe I don't deserve love.* My brain is mush. Pure turmoil. I cry out to God. *Why am I alone? Will I never get over not being married?*

My mother tells me quite often that I allow men to use me. That I have a history of getting attached and committing to someone who doesn't want long-term. Then, after the guy takes everything I have to offer without doing the right thing (putting a ring on it), I am abandoned. I am left feeling old, worn, and dirty. I gave away the milk for free, and now all that is left is a bit of spilled milk from an unbought cow that's been sucked dry.

Most of the time I disagree with my mother's horribly negative comments. But at times I look at my scars and feel she's a little justified. I have baggage that weighs me down. I feel abandoned and unwanted, like an afterthought or a second-hand coat bought at a thrift store just for rainy days. I am that worn jacket stuffed in a closet, waiting for "maybe, future, later" – not a legitimate part of the wardrobe to be shown off and valued.

And now, all I can do, all any of us can do, is hope and pray things get better.

Maybe I am "used". Maybe I am scarred. I don't know what to do to make them fade. Maybe I feel like crying or dying or running away from my responsibilities. My life is a romantic comedy that needs a miraculous happy ending, but I don't think it will happen. No one is chasing after me, telling me not to get on a plane, or not to marry the other guy, because he can't live without me. Yeah, I have some scars that are causing major problems.

But I'm never going to give up, because I'm a Warrior.

I am so proud of my friend Nichole Peters. She has overcome so much and told me her incredible story. She has been passionate about her goals to be a great writer and publisher, and she has taken so many strides and has grown so much as an author since I met her. Even when obstacles come her way, like her original publishing company (the one I used to work for), trying to take advantage of her, or people stealing and plagiarizing her work, and others not keeping their promises, Nichole is a class act. She is tenacious and she is animated. She becomes determined to work harder and do better and demand more, because she Warriors Up!

These women and their testimonies have inspired me to fight my demons and battle my inner darkness. I have learned from their stories to love myself despite my scars, because I survived abuse and abandonment. I can live, prosper, and love even with the scars. I just need to fight the darkness, and to hope.

Sometimes I Hate Hope

However, I never doubt the stubbornness of Hope… She refuses to be forgotten. Hope is the queen of rebirth, of revival, of reincarnation. Since Pandora left Hope alone in a jar, she has fought to be heard. Hope encourages the underdog; she hates those "should'ves, could'ves, would'ves." Hope is a balm to your raw soul and whispers assurances that hold back dejected tears. Crap may float and Hope eventually drowns, but rather than stay in her watery grave, Hope rises again to the surface to give birth to a renaissance.

Sometimes I hate Hope… but I can't help but think, would good things in this world exist without that annoying emotion dogging my every step? Hope keeps telling me to wait for "One day…"

Claudia Alexander

Claudia is a public school teacher, author, editor and tutor who loves a good challenge. As a minister's daughter, Claudia feels she has been cursed with a rebellious spirit and a good heart. Claudia is a mother of one beautiful child and hopes to make a living one day writing full time. For more information, reach out on Facebook or check out her website @ http://www.metisrise.com/

Dedication

This book is dedicated to the amazing Angel in heaven watching over me. My grandmother Essie, better known as "Mamma," absolutely loved all her grandchildren, but I was around her more than most. From the time I was born to my first day of college, we lived ALL our lives together in the same household because Ma'Dear took care of her nine children along with her mother.

My grandmother used to talk to me for countless hours while we sat on the hot concrete steps in the projects called Redmond Heights. She was my other-mother. She was my heart. My grandmother's bloodline was half Cherokee Indian. She inherited a very humble but strong spiritual presence that I believe shaped me also.

I hid for years how I suffered in grief, missing her so much after she passed away. She was the iron that sharpened my spine when the enemy was trying to break it. Father God, I thank you for sending me such a loving spirit to show me how to fight evil and be a warrior. Rest in peace, Beautiful. I will see you again!

Readers, before the closing of this book, I want to share this story on how Nikki-Woman, my spiritual avatar, came to be and relate the words of Essie Peters to the world. Here goes...

Here comes Nikki-Woman

Most days, before the sun went down, I would sit on the front porch to clear my mind. It was hard sometimes, even in the sunshine, to think good thoughts when darkness was haunting you, but every once in a while, I had some dreams that weren't dark. Now this may seem a little strange, but when I think about those not-so-dark dreams, I felt amazingly powerful. As a thirteen-year-old child, I imagined I was a superhero. I pictured a beautiful woman, like Mamma, dressed in a Wonder Woman outfit. There was this strange overflowing feeling that I'd help save a lot of people in this cold-hearted world one day soon.

Wonder Nikki's outfit was fit for a warrior. It glowed and came with some major powers. Her breastplate was made out of 100% steel, and instead of Wonder Woman's rope lasso, Wonder Nikki had powerful swords that could take anybody down. With every win against the enemy, Wonder Nikki grew stronger and stronger. Whenever she helped someone escape danger, Wonder Nikki would gain more power. If the demons came out with an evil Super Woman, it still wouldn't stop the superhero Wonder Nikki. She was just unbelievable and unstoppable!!! I sincerely believe Wonder Nikki, aka Nikki-Woman, represented God's strength inside me. 1 John 4:4 (NLV) says, "But you belong to God, my dear children. You have already won a victory over those people, because the Spirit who lives in you is greater than the spirit who lives in the world." Nobody could stop her from saving the world; even satan had to flee and bow down!

The good thing was, these superhero dreams often followed the horrific demonic nightmares. Every once in a while, I'd wake up with a smile on my face and feel refreshed. Even thinking about the Wonder Nikki dreams made me feel better and more alive. So I sat on the front porch, absorbing the sunlight, thinking about steel and swords, and for those few moments, I forgot the voice, the enemy, and the nightmares. I would hear Father God say, "For you have been a protector, a strong tower from the enemy."

Mamma could tell when I was troubled. One day she stopped me from getting up. "Baby girl, don't leave off the porch yet. I need to have a serious talk with you." She got up out of the chair and came to the screen door, then my grandmother told me something I'd never forget.

"I know sometimes you didn't understand why I was stricter on you than some of the others. You are your mother, my daughter Effie's, unique child. Even when you were a baby and couldn't walk yet, you would never give up. You would get up and fall down so many times and bump your head, over and over again." Mamma smiled at me through the porch screen.

"You see, Nikki, every baby falls down when they're trying to walk, but some will keep crying and will stop trying, some will wait and try again later, especially after getting knots on their heads. But there are ones who are very rare. They jump up immediately after every fall." She looked me dead in the eyes and said, "You are one of them babies that kept jumping up, Nikki. You were trying to stand up when it wasn't even your time yet. Instead of crawling, you were trying your best to walk. So I already knew, since you were a baby, you were going to be something special. You were born to be somebody. I want to see your dreams get lived out. Never let anybody tell you that you can't do it, because you weren't made that way. You were made to carry out your dreams, Nikki. I always saw the Fighter in you. I see it now, even when you don't."

After hearing the Father God's voice and Mamma's words, along with the sunlight, the positive superhero dreams, and me being safe at home, gave me strength. I felt the darkness retreat a little. I started feeling a little better. It was easier to really appreciate life, no matter what was going on, because I knew I was born to do some extraordinary things.

Remembering those words from my grandmother still brings a smile to my face and a few tears to my eyes. I am a Warrior because I stand my ground, I'm not afraid to fight, and because I have inherited the strength to get back up again immediately after I fall. **I LOVE YOU, MAMMA!!!**

Nichole Peters

She is an international motivational speaker, CEO, and founder of Women of Love, Power, and Respect, Women Warriors Who Makes It ROCK, and Believe In Your Dreams Publishing. Nichole is the producer of The Motivational Lounge, an upcoming radio show powered by Voice-America and the bestselling author of *A Woman of Love, Power, & Respect*. She believes in nurturing beautiful souls. Determined to teach downtrodden women and youths the power of self-love, Nichole facilitates workshops and social media coaching for organizations, conferences, and churches, which encourages people to claim their blessings and live up to their greatness within. In the last decade, Nichole has witnessed MANIFESTATION like never before.

The youngest of nine children, Nichole was born and raised in a small town called Bogalusa, Louisiana (63 miles north of New Orleans). Nichole has experienced many hardships in life, but has never lost hope that she would one day serve a greater purpose. As a result, God has not only blessed her with four amazing, beautiful children, but He brought her the love of her life in 2005 and revealed to her the potential to be a writer.

Nichole remains a five-star author on Amazon and Barnes & Noble. Nichole is also a wellness and beauty advocate. She is also a die-hard advocate for domestic violence survivors. Nichole reaches out to different safe houses for abused women and delivers a message to let every woman know "they are beautiful, strong, and can live off true love, not abuse." Nichole has two channels on *Empowered ConnectionsTV*™, powered by Voice-America, but on January 20, 2017, Nichole will launch her own Believe In Your Dreams network channel powered by RHG Media.

"I have always loved God, but as a youth, I never truly embraced his teachings. In 2010, I decided to put HIM first in my Life. I promised God that no matter what storms I came across, no matter what the enemy tried to do... this would be our New Beginning and I would NEVER stop giving Him praise, no matter what. I will NEVER GIVE UP AGAIN!"

www.believeinyourdreamspublishing.com
www.facebook.com/luvpowerrespect
www.Twitter.com/luvpowerrespect
believeinyourdreamsproductions@gmail.com

47687863R00133

Made in the USA
San Bernardino, CA
09 April 2017